THE GREAT
CORNISH
FISH BOOK

A feast of recipes, tales and discoveries from
Cornwall's coastal larder

Written and edited by Ruth Huxley and Rosie Willmot
Designed by Design Room Cornwall Ltd
Principal designer: Emma Gordon
Principal photographer: Sally Mitchell
Research and contributing copywriters: Dave Huxley and Kevin Gray-Roberts
Contributing photographers: Sean Gee and Kate Whitaker
Contributing illustrator/designer: Heather Allen
Other illustration: Seafish; Nicole Heidaripour (John Dory, page 134);
                    Sarah McCartney (crab, front cover)

THE GREAT CORNISH FISH BOOK
A Design Room Cornwall production on behalf of Cornwall Food & Drink Ltd
Published by: Cornwall Food & Drink Ltd
Printed by: Fourway Print Ltd, Launceston, Cornwall

PAGE 154 ORIGINAL RECIPE FROM NATHAN OUTLAW'S FISH KITCHEN
(QUADRILLE, £20) PHOTO © DAVID LOFTUS
PAGE 86 RECIPE © JACK STEIN
PAGE 88-89 PHOTO © SEAFISH
CRAB ILLUSTRATION (FRONT COVER) © CORNWALL WILDLIFE TRUST
OTHER FISH AND SHELLFISH ILLUSTRATIONS © SEAFISH

Cornwall Food & Drink

CONTENTS

FOREWORD

There was a memorable sketch in Monty Python's Flying Circus about a counterfeit British Ambassador in the city of Smolensk who was, in fact, a Chinaman. He claimed his parents had come from Cornwall. Being Chinese, (played by Graham Chapman) he couldn't pronounce the word. He kept saying *Caranoilwall.* Michael Palin was an earnest Cornishman in khaki shorts called Mr Pither who was seeking assistance in getting back home. Cornwall has just the right mixture of difficult syllables. *Caranoilwall.* Whenever I think about writing something serious about Cornwall that sketch resurfaces and I can't help laughing. It's irrelevant when thinking about the way the county has become an internationally well-regarded part of the UK for great food and wine. But in a sense it's not a complete non sequitur, the joke in the sketch was slightly that Cornwall was a rather remote place where not even a bogus ambassador's parents would come from. That's not true anymore. I'm also using the thought because Cornwall makes me smile, makes everyone smile who comes here. I'm looking out of my office window now and seeing happy and contented tourists. Everyone loves Cornwall and more and more the food and drink in the Royal Duchy is worth a visit in its own right let alone the dramatic cliffs and long sandy beaches.

Culinary Cornwall has been transformed in the last 40 odd years and I am very proud to have been part of the transformation, but the foundation to that has always been here. It's the quality of the raw materials and a determination by a growing band of enthusiasts to tell the world about it. It's one thing to have great fish, dairy produce, meat, fruit and vegetables on your doorstep but quite another

to shout it from the rooftops. That has been done by ever improving cooking and a continuing skill in catching and keeping the best quality fish and shellfish, in growing better produce and rearing contented livestock, brewing great beer and making characterful cheeses. Running with this has been an extraordinary growth in selling the whole idea of Cornwall as a special place for eating and drinking, not least the organisation which champions local food and produce, Cornwall Food and Drink. So in the fortieth anniversary of opening The Seafood Restaurant I say - here's to *Caranoilwall.*

RICK STEIN, AUGUST 2015

It's almost impossible to think of Cornwall without conjuring up images of the coastline and the sea. Granite harbours, rugged clifftops, crashing waves, golden sands. Unsurprising really, in this peninsula where you're never further than 20 miles from the coast, and most of the time very much closer.

Thousands of people in Cornwall depend on that same sea and coastline for their living, and none more so than the fishermen who carve out a demanding existence from it, never knowing what the next day might bring or whether they will survive it. It's a way of life on which whole communities depend too. And it's one of the cornerstones of a culinary reputation that brings people from all over the world to this beautiful sliver of land at England's most westerly tip. We touched upon this in The Great Cornish Food Book but knew that there was much more to tell, worthy of a book in its own right. Two years later, this is that book.

Cornwall's reputation for producing and serving great seafood hasn't come about simply by virtue of being a place surrounded by the sea. A combination of factors creates a unique marine environment that attracts a colossal variety of fish and shellfish to these shores, which in turn sustains a larger fleet of small fishing boats than anywhere else in Britain. These are the guys who are catching and handling the fish in ways that not only retain its quality and freshness but are also highly sustainable.

It's a way of fishing that almost died out during the second half of the last century and many people blame the amount of 'factory fishing' that took place off-shore. Delve a bit deeper and it's clear that this was yet another episode in fishing's centuries-old tendency to swing from boom to bust, as different types of fishery evolved and were then fished almost to extinction.

Right now there is a new dawn in fishing that is breaking that cycle, and Cornwall is right up there blazing the trail. Management of the oceans, although widely grumbled about and certainly not without its issues, is acknowledged as a necessary evil

these days and even welcomed by a new breed of fishermen, merchants, fishmongers and chefs who all depend on a sustainable fishery for their living and want to see it survive into the future. These are the people who are also grasping the opportunity to think differently about how fish is sold, and some of their stories and insights are here for you to read.

The way we buy and eat seafood is part of the transformation too. Until I married a man who knew his way around fish, I confess I was someone who loved seafood but didn't really know where to begin with it in my own kitchen. So I made do with fish that I could find easily and deal with comfortably, which generally meant it came out of the freezer cabinet in a packet. In the intervening 20 years, my eyes have been opened to a variety I just didn't know existed and I've even discovered the thrill of catching and cooking my own supper (and outfishing my own husband!). Fresh mackerel, in the pan within hours of being hooked, takes some serious beating.

The chefs who have shared their seafood recipes in this book will say that Cornish fish is some of the best in the world and the reason many of them are here. It's much easier to get hold of these days too because it doesn't all head automatically overseas in the way it did for many years. So whether you're a seasoned pro looking for some new ideas, a newbie to seafood in need of inspiration, or you just love Cornwall, I hope this book will inspire you to dive in and get hooked.

RUTH HUXLEY
Founder and Director of Cornwall Food & Drink

FISH EVERY DAY

When it comes to speedy prep, adaptable flavours and all-round nutrition, few could argue that fish is the dish that ticks all the boxes. However, Britain's never really got the hang of fish in the way you'd expect from an island nation that adores the seaside - on average, we eat just one portion per person per week, and over a third of the fish we buy is ready-prepared or pre-packed.

The winds of change are definitely blowing and more people are eager to be adventurous with seafood. A revival of fishmongers, on the high street and on the web, means it's becoming more straightforward to get hold of a wide variety of really fresh, top quality catch. But with heads, tails, bones and scales to worry about, isn't it all a bit too much like hard work? With a helpful fishmonger, definitely not. Online or in person, they will make it easy for you - it's what they're trained for, and they love it.

All the recipes in this chapter have been given the thumbs up for ease of preparation and passed the taste test of both children and adults. They'll make swift midweek meals but are definitely tasty enough for something special too. They are also all adaptable to whatever type of fish is available so don't worry too much about sticking rigorously to the suggested species either.

WHAT TO BUY WHEN?

With so much choice and lots of different factors to take into account, it's not always an easy question to answer. You'll find most types of fish to some extent throughout the year but there are definitely optimum times to choose different species in order to keep fish stocks healthy and to get the best taste and quality. However, because fish habits and habitats are affected by the weather and sea conditions – as is the fishing – it can be a tricky old business trying to categorically define the availability of fish from one season to the next.

Rob Wing is a fish merchant and online fishmonger who started his working life as a chef then spent time at sea as a fisherman before becoming a merchant, and now also a Newlyn Harbour Commissioner. With his understanding of fish from every angle, his rule of thumb is to work with nature – avoid the breeding seasons and buy according to what's abundant – which will usually mean you're eating it at its best and also landing the best value.

ROB'S TOP TIPS FOR BUYING FISH

BUY LOCAL

Buy as close to the source as possible. The less a fish has been handled or travelled, the better it will be and the more you will be able to find out about it.

BUY DIFFERENT

Buy something different every time you go into the fishmonger's. The more variety of fish we eat, the less pressure there will be on stocks.

BUY WHOLE

Always buy a whole fish if you can. The fishmonger will fillet it for you if you need. Ask for the bones if you want to make your own stock.

BUY FRESH

Today's catch!

If it looks fresh, it probably is. But look for bright eyes, firm flesh, red gills and a sweet smell. Fresh fish doesn't smell fishy.

SARDINE
September - March

DOVER SOLE
All year

RED MULLET
January - September

LEMON SOLE
March - November

MEGRIM
All Year

KNOW YOUR FISH

MUSSEL
Wild: September - April
Farmed: All year

MONKFISH
All year

BLACK BREAM
All year (intermittently)

SCALLOP
All year

BASS
December - March

BROWN CRAB
March - November

LOBSTER
March - October

TURBOT
May - July

RED GURNARD
All year

MACKEREL
September - March

HAKE
All year

Some of the many species found around the coasts of Cornwall and the Isles of Scilly and our guide to the best time to buy them.

POLLACK
January - April

COD
May - December

HERRING
September - March

JOHN DORY
June - August

RAZOR CLAM
May - September

BRILL
October - May

SQUID
September - January

SPIDER CRAB
March - May
October - November

NATIVE OYSTER
November - March

WHAT'S FOR TEA?

Packed with protein, vitamins, minerals and brainpower-boosting Omegas, fish is a superfood for growing kids, but they can often be reluctant to give it a try. Someone who reckons she's cracked it when it comes to making fish a food her whole family tucks into is Tor Amran. Tor runs the Cornish Food Box Company with her sister Lucy and switched to making fish a regular feature in family meals when they started adding fresh fish boxes to their weekly rounds.

The catch of the week comes straight from Mousehole and, because they never know what they'll be getting, Tor devised a collection of easily adaptable recipes. Her fishfingers, made with a few simple, natural ingredients, are her sons' favourite and a winner with every big and little person who tries them.

Making your own means much more fish in each finger than the ones that come out of a packet and they can be made using any type of fresh white fish. Tor's family love them made with hake because of its firm meaty texture and fine flavour.

DON'T LIKE FISH? Give it another go - scientists say people need to try a new food up to 10 times before their taste buds come to like it.

FISHFINGERS

Tor Amran, Cornish Food Box Company, Truro

INGREDIENTS Serves a family of 4

4 fillets of chunky fresh white fish -
hake, cod, haddock, pollack, whiting
or gurnard are ideal

2 free range eggs

4-5 slices fresh white bread

A handful of sieved plain flour

Sunflower or Cornish rapeseed oil
for frying

Cornish sea salt and black pepper

METHOD

- Blitz the bread slices in a food processor to make fine breadcrumbs. Season and put in a wide bowl.
- Beat both eggs in another wide bowl.
- Using a sharp knife, preferably a fish knife, remove the skin from the fish and make sure any remaining bones are removed. Cut the fish into long pieces - any size you like.
- Pour the flour into a third wide bowl. You will need enough to coat each piece of fish.
- Get the kids to coat the fish - first in the flour, followed by the egg, followed by the breadcrumbs. Things will get messy!
- Heat enough oil to cover the base of a wide pan and add the fishfingers. Fry until golden brown over a medium high heat, first on one side, then the other.
- Eat straight away. Try serving in a wrap with fresh salad and mayonnaise for something a bit different.

FISH 'N TIPS TOR'S TOP TIPS FOR GETTING
KIDS TO TRY FISH, AND LIKE IT

1. Keep it simple. Use filleted fish to start with to avoid any issues with bones.
2. Get little hands helping - the more they can get involved, the more they'll be willing to try the end result.
3. Don't be afraid of the mess – it's all part of the fun.
4. Allow kids to suggest their own recipe variations. They can be surprisingly good.
5. Be positive about what they have eaten and don't go on about what they haven't.

CORNISH CRAB & HADDOCK BURGER

Chris Gordon & Kristian Fleming, The Cornish Ketchup Company

A speedy Friday night supper that packs all the flavour and zing of the Cornish coastline, from the guys who really know their condiments.

INGREDIENTS Serves 4

FOR THE BURGER

250g Cornish haddock fillets

100g Cornish white crab meat

175ml dry white wine

Juice of $\frac{1}{2}$ a lemon

1 egg (to bind)

$\frac{1}{2}$ tsp Cornish sea salt

Black pepper

FOR THE CRISP CRUMB

100g toasted sourdough breadcrumbs

50g grated parmesan cheese

Zest of 1 unwaxed lemon

Rapeseed oil (for frying)

METHOD

- Place the haddock fillets in a medium pan with the white wine and gently poach for 5 minutes. Drain and set aside to cool.

- Put the cooked haddock into a bowl, flake it up and add the crab meat, lemon juice, sea salt and a pinch of black pepper. Add the egg and mix well.

- On a large plate, mix together the grated parmesan cheese, lemon zest and breadcrumbs.

- Separate the burger mix into four portions, roll each portion in the crumb mix and form a burger shape with your hands - this can get quite messy.

- Cover the base of a large frying pan with rapeseed oil and heat on a medium to high setting. With a fish slice gently lift the burgers up and tap away any excess crumbs. Fry for 2 minutes on each side or until golden. Remove from the pan and drain on kitchen paper.

- Serve on a toasted brioche burger bun with a handful of watercress and a good dollop of Red Pepper Ketchup.

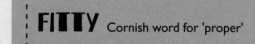

FITTY Cornish word for 'proper'

Over 3,500 tonnes
of crab are landed at
Cornish ports each year,
worth over £5 million
to Cornwall's
economy.

DOING YOU

GOOD

Fish is one of the healthiest things to eat and white fish, oily fish and shellfish are all superfoods in their own way. Aim for at least two portions a week, one of which should be an oily fish, and feel the benefit.

LOVE YOUR

The low saturated fats and high Omega-3 fatty acids in fish can help reduce blood cholesterol and protect the heart from disease.

KEEP IN

White fish is high in protein but low in fat, just the job for feeling fuller for longer without piling on the calories.

STAY

The Omega-3 in oily fish can keep joints healthy and fish that you eat whole contain calcium and phosphorous for strong bones.

FEEL

The combination of nutrients in seafood can improve concentration and brainpower and help keep depression at bay.

GET

Rich in many of the essential micronutrients plus vitamins A, D, E and K, seafood keeps the body tuned up and the immune system strong.

LOOK

Keep skin radiant with collagen-building protein and Omega-3 to protect from UV damage. Eating fish can help conditions like eczema and psoriasis too.

Fish is a star ingredient. Quick and versatile, it's a no-brainer for those times when you're hungry and tired and need refuelling in a hurry with no messing about.

FUSS-FREE
☆ FISH ☆

A FEW POINTERS FOR PLAIN SAILING

1. Above all, find a friendly fishmonger. Scaling, gutting, skinning and filleting are a walk in the park for them. They will also be able to suggest substitutes if a particular fish you're looking for isn't around.

2. You can buy hand-picked Cornish crab and lobster meat either in person or online direct from the processors as well as from fishmongers. Keep some in the freezer – it defrosts quickly and can be added to dishes or made into a luxurious sandwich in a flash.

3. Smaller fish like mackerel, herrings and sardines don't need to be gutted if you're going to be using them as fillets. Simply cut the fillets from the bone and discard everything else.

4. For no-mess coatings, put flour in a plastic bag, add seasoning, drop the fillets in, give it a shake, remove the fillets, job done.

5. When making fish stock, make a little more than you need and freeze the excess in ice cube trays once it's chilled. Defrost just as much as you need to give a natural lift to seafood sauces and soups.

6. Simmer a few slices of lemon or lime in a pan with the lid off to freshen up the kitchen after frying fish.

NO FAFF FISH PIE

Annie Sibert, My Fish Kitchen,
Mawnan Smith

A fishmonger for 25 years who now runs her own seafood cookery school, Annie is also a busy mum so she's created plenty of fish recipes that can be put together in a flash. This one is her own family's absolute favourite, made with minimal ingredients and good value fish.

INGREDIENTS Serves 4

1kg Cornish floury potatoes

100g Cornish salted butter

430ml Cornish milk

1kg Cornish pollack fillets, skinned

400ml water

1 large onion, roughly chopped

150g Cornish mature cheddar cheese

METHOD

- Make the mashed potato by boiling the potatoes, then draining and adding the butter and a good splash of milk. Cream the ingredients well with a masher or ricer.
- Pour the remaining milk into a medium saucepan with the water and the chopped onion. Heat until it's just beginning to bubble, add the pollack fillets, leaving them whole. Simmer for 2-3 minutes, depending on the thickness of the fish. When the flakes separate easily, it's cooked.
- Transfer the fish to an ovenproof dish with the onion and some of the juices from the pan. Don't be tempted to break up the fish fillets - pollack will flake really well as it cooks. Grate the cheese and sprinkle it over the top of the mixture. Gently cover the cheese with spoonfuls of the mashed potato.
- Place the dish under the grill for 4 minutes until the potato is browned.
- Serve straight away with a seasonal green veg or frozen peas.

FISH 'N TIPS

This pie can easily be made in a batch and frozen after cooling. Defrost overnight and reheat for 25 minutes in the oven at 160°C.

Ling is an alternative fish for this dish and is equally good value, but doesn't flake as easily, so will need cutting into pieces. It has a bit less flavour than pollack too so may need a bit of salt.

To add a touch of luxury, add a few scallops a minute before you add the fish to the mixture in the pan.

THE LINK IN THE CHAIN

Watching a fishmonger wield a razor-sharp knife with mesmerizing speed is awesome stuff. For many, it's a skill they grew up with, watching and learning as their parents worked the family fish counter.

Nearly always, the fishing link is generations-old. In Looe, the Pengelly family started selling fresh fish in the 1960s, from a handheld cart they hawked around the town, eventually setting up a static counter on the quayside. Sisters Angela and Jackie, whose father and grandfather fished for a living, keep the family tradition alive these days, running one of the busiest, buzziest, cheeriest fishmongers you'll ever come across. With the market on their doorstep, they have the pick of the catch from the Looe and Polperro day boat fleet every morning.

Further west in the harbour town of Penryn, David Seabourne is part of the high-street revival of independent traders. Like the Pengellys, Seabourne Fish also started out on wheels, in David's case venturing into the back of beyond to run weekly deliveries of freshly-caught seafood to Cornwall's rural villages. After recognising that more and more people are keen to try new types of fish and to buy it more often, he's recently taken the plunge and set up his own bricks and mortar shop in Penryn, with a fish counter chock full each day with seasonal seafood bought from local fishing boats and Newlyn market. But he's not getting rid of his wheels; in fact he now has three vans that cover a big chunk of mid and west Cornwall.

CORNISH SARDINES

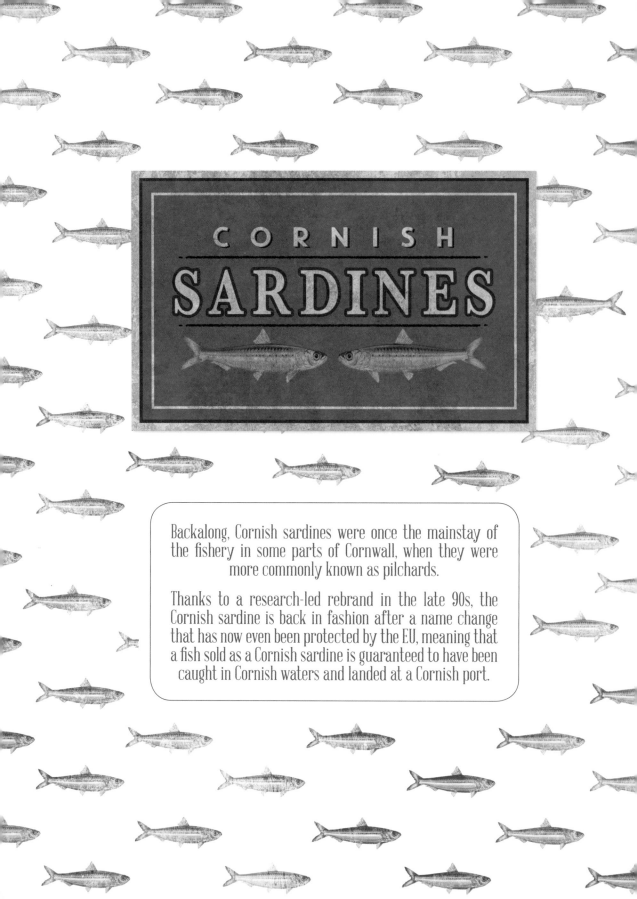

Backalong, Cornish sardines were once the mainstay of the fishery in some parts of Cornwall, when they were more commonly known as pilchards.

Thanks to a research-led rebrand in the late 90s, the Cornish sardine is back in fashion after a name change that has now even been protected by the EU, meaning that a fish sold as a Cornish sardine is guaranteed to have been caught in Cornish waters and landed at a Cornish port.

MRS T'S CORNISH SARDINES

Valerie Thomson, Falmouth Bay Seafood Café, Truro

Cornish sardines are tasty, inexpensive, quick to cook and very good for you. For the best flavour, buy them fresh when they're in season. Val's recipe makes a lovely supper or lunch.

INGREDIENTS Serves 4

8 whole fresh Cornish sardines, scaled and gutted

I red onion, finely chopped

I clove garlic, crushed

125ml white wine

50g baby capers

8 cherry tomatoes, chopped

3 bay leaves

2 tbsp plain flour

Cornish sea salt and ground back pepper

2 tbsp extra virgin olive oil, plus extra for frying

METHOD

- Heat 2 tablespoons of the oil in a large frying pan over medium heat. Add the onion and garlic, and cook for 5 minutes or until soft.

- Add wine, capers, tomatoes and bay leaves, and season with salt and pepper.

- Turn the heat down and let the sauce simmer for 10 minutes, stirring occasionally until it has thickened and reduced down.

- Put the flour with some salt and pepper in a plastic bag and toss the sardines in the mixture, then shake off any excess.

- Place enough oil in a frying pan to coat the bottom of the pan, add the sardines in a single layer and cook over a medium heat for about 3 minutes on each side, just until the fish are nicely golden.

- Transfer the sardines onto some kitchen towel to remove excess oil, then pop them in a serving dish. Garnish the dish with the tomato and caper sauce, top with parsley and serve with fresh bread, lemon wedges and green salad leaves.

TOOLS OF THE TRADE

Despite the variety of seafood available, you might be surprised to find that a sharp filleting knife and a decent board are usually all fishmongers rely on for most of what they do. That doesn't mean that there isn't plenty of gadgetry for any seafood enthusiast to invest in if they fancy, but it's easy to get started with a few basics and there are plenty of ways to improvise by using what you've got at home.

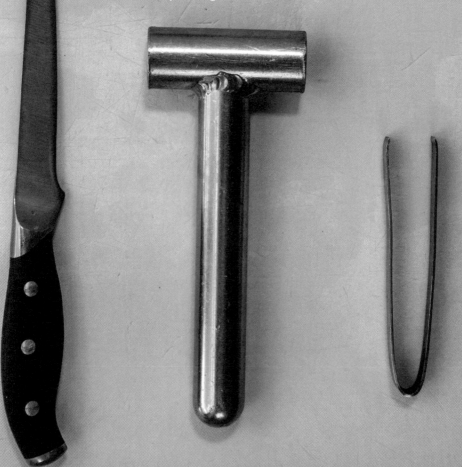

DESCALING TOOL

Most fishmongers will descale fish automatically for you, or do it on request. If you're catching your own or buying direct from fishermen, it's a job you'll need to tackle yourself. The simple tools you can buy are inexpensive and make quick work of any size fish, but the back of a knife will do the trick too.

FILLETING KNIFE

For best results, choose a knife with a long, thin blade that has a bit of flex to it and a comfortable handle.

MALLET

For cracking crab and lobster shells. A rolling pin makes a great alternative, or try a clean pair of mole grips – you can exert just enough pressure without sending fragments everywhere.

TWEEZERS

For pin-boning, which makes all the difference to eating quality. Industrial tweezers will stand up to regular use and the dishwasher, but cosmetic ones will work just fine.

· · · · · · · · · · · · · OTHER HANDY GADGETS · · · · · · · · · · · · ·

SHARPENING STEEL

A knife is useless if it isn't sharp - investing in a decent steel and learning how to use it properly is a wise move.

PICKING TOOL

A long thin pick will help you get all the flesh from the legs and claws of crab and lobster, but some professional fishmongers swear that a teaspoon handle does this just as well.

SHUCKING KNIFE

If you're using fresh oysters, you need to find a way of opening them without losing all the juices from the inside while making sure your oyster stays free of shell splinters. A shucking knife, which has a short pointed blade and a stop to prevent your fingers slipping into it, is really helpful.

SHELLFISHING

With no fishing quotas attached to shellfish, and Cornish waters an attractive habitat for crab and lobster, it's hardly surprising that potting is big business in Cornwall. Worth millions each year, it's time-honoured fishing too. The design and materials of the pots may have moved on, but the method is the same as it's always been. With no bycatch or discards to worry about (any undersize or poor quality specimens are simply returned to the sea alive) and minimal impact on the seafloor habitat, this is about as sustainable as it gets.

Around the north coast of Cornwall, from ports like Newquay and Padstow and the chocolate-box harbour of Port Isaac, there's a high concentration of shellfishing. It's an awkward journey from many of these places to the traditional fish markets on the south coast, so selling the catch direct to the seriously good seafood chefs on their doorstep and a local wholesaler who exports live Cornish shellfish all over the world makes a lot of sense.

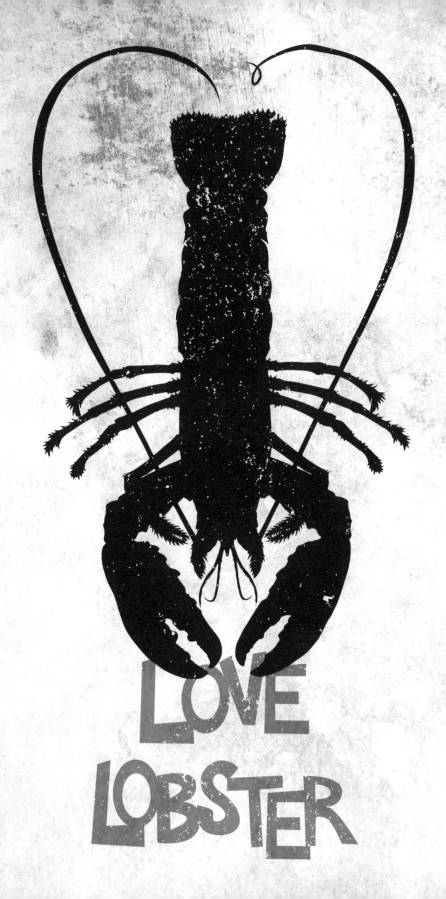

LOVE
LOBSTER

⇧ UPPING THE ODDS ⇧

While Cornish seas may leave swimmers shivering, the hardy European lobster just loves the Atlantic chill. It's said that colder waters mean more flavour too, so while many of the Southern European countries might enjoy the warmth of the Med, they often turn to Cornwall for supplies of this highly-prized and most delectable shellfish.

With lobsters fetching good prices, they are an attractive catch for fishermen too. However, lobsters are definitely not the rabbits of the shellfish world. They take five to eight years to reach maturity and a female mates on average once every two years, after which only one of her 20,000 eggs is expected to make it to adulthood - most simply get hoovered up by hungry predators soon after they are released.

THE NATIONAL LOBSTER HATCHERY AT PADSTOW

runs an ingenious research and conservation programme aimed at giving nature a helping hand to enhance lobster stocks. It's pretty impressive, and this is how it works...

When local fishermen catch berried (egg-bearing) hen lobsters, they take them to the hatchery.

The eggs hatch and the mothers are returned to the sea by the fishermen.

The larvae are reared in a controlled communal environment at the hatchery.

The developing lobsters are then separated into individual compartments until they become juveniles – at around three months old.

The fishermen release the juveniles back into the sea, where one in twenty is expected to survive.

The conservation programme at the Lobster Hatchery improves the survival rate 1000 fold

FROM POT TO PLATE

Calum Greenhalgh is a shellfisherman based at Port Isaac. Unusually, Calum is a first generation fisherman who was brought up in the heart of England and didn't get to know the coast until he headed to university in Plymouth. There he met his wife Tracey, whose fisherman father gave Calum his first taste of what it's like to earn a living from the sea and got him hooked. Calum now skippers his own boat and he and Tracey run Fresh from the Sea, an all-in-one deli, café and fishmonger they set up in the village in 2009, with the aim of adding a bit more value to their catch.

Lobster + Crab from our boat to your plate

TACKLING A LIVE LOBSTER

KNOWN FOR THEIR FRESHER-THAN-FRESH LOBSTER AND CRAB SANDWICHES AND SALADS, THIS IS CALUM AND TRACEY'S GUIDE TO THE TASK THEY KNOW MANY PEOPLE FIND DAUNTING – DEALING WITH A LIVE LOBSTER

1. Make sure you have a saucepan large enough to take your whole lobster.

2. Fill $1/3$ to $1/2$ full with fresh water. Some people suggest the water should be salty but Calum reckons the lobster is salty enough without.

3. Pop the live lobster in the freezer for 10 minutes while you bring the water to the boil. This makes the lobster sleepy.

4. When the water is boiling vigorously, put the lobster in the pan and bring the water back to the boil.

5. Turn the heat down and simmer the lobster for 10-20 minutes, according to size and how you like your lobster meat. The longer you cook it, the softer it will get. The cooked lobster will have turned the classic pinky orange colour (the shell of the European lobster is dark blue when it's alive).

6. Remove the lobster from the water and allow it to cool, then leave it to chill in the fridge. If you try to pick the meat without doing this you will lose lots of the juice and end up with dry meat.

7. Now to get the meat out. Chop the lobster in half lengthways by following the white line you will see running down the top of the shell, a bit like a parting.

8. Remove and discard the stomach sac, which you will find directly underneath the eyes, about the size of a finger nail.

9. The meat should lift out. Remove the dark intestinal vein from the tail (there may not be one) with the point of a sharp knife, but you don't need to remove the gills – it's a fallacy that lobster gills are poisonous.

10. Keep the grey meat (this is the liver and is known as the tomalley), which can be used to make a delicious lobster mayonnaise.

11. Use a sharp knife to cut the big part of each claw in half, then dig out the meat. The other claw joints should just snap in half.

12. Use straight away for the freshest, tastiest lobster ever. In the unlikely event that you don't finish it in one sitting, pop the rest in the freezer.

FISHING FOR TOMORROW

Fifth generation Padstow fisherman, Johnny Murt, grew up with shellfishing and will talk happily about how much his grandad, his father and his uncles taught him. However, Johnny's other love was always sport and it was his talent on the football pitch that, after an initial spell at sea when he left school, landed him a scholarship and the chance to hop more than 3,000 miles across the pond to study in Massachusetts. There, he was able to build on that handed-down family wisdom with a degree, then a Masters and lab research, all helping to shape a deep understanding of the factors determining fisheries conservation and development.

"My grandad is constantly making and repairing gear for me and handing out advice - to everyone - whether wanted or not!"

Eventually, the pull of Padstow proved too much and he returned, buying and renovating his own boat, Homarus, to fish for crab and lobster between Trevose Head and Port Isaac in time-honoured Murt fashion. Anyone lucky enough to chat to Johnny for more than a few minutes will realise that this is a man whose extraordinary knowledge and love of the sea, not to mention a decade's experience from another continent and boundless ideas, are helping to ensure that future generations have a productive industry to work in.

JOHNNY AND RICK ARE AMONG THE SHELLFISHERMEN, FISHMONGERS, MERCHANTS AND RESTAURANTS WHO SUPPORT THE LOBSTER HATCHERY'S BUY ONE SET ONE FREE SCHEME, MAKING A DONATION FOR EACH LOBSTER SOLD.

THE NATIONAL LOBSTER HATCHERY
BUY ONE
SET ONE FREE!

CORNISH LOBSTER CARPACCIO

Rick Toogood, Prawn on the Lawn, Padstow

Joining the list of talented chefs who have made their way to Cornwall, Rick's fresh fish counter and seafood bar combo is the latest addition to Padstow's booming food scene. Johnny Murt supplies him with crab and lobster for Prawn on the Lawn in both Padstow and Islington.

INGREDIENTS Serves 2

1 cooked Cornish lobster, around 1kg

200g medium sized asparagus spears

10 nasturtium leaves, or finely sliced radish

10 Peruvian marigold leaves, or finely sliced apple

10 micro-fennel leaves, or fennel tops

Juice of $\frac{1}{2}$ a lemon

Edible flowers, e.g. rose petals, borage

Cracked black pepper

Cornish sea salt

Dulse flakes, or fresh samphire

METHOD

- Remove the meat from the lobster, following the instructions on page 35, and cut the tail meat and the claw meat into thin slices.
- Remove the grey meat from the lobster body, add a quarter of the lemon juice and a little salt and pepper. Whisk up and set aside.
- Bring a saucepan of water to the boil and add a pinch of salt. Bend the asparagus, and where it snaps discard the woody bottom bits - you are then left with the edible part. Once the water is boiling, add the asparagus tips and, after just 20-30 seconds, remove and plunge into iced water – this shocks them, keeping their colour and crunch. Using a vegetable peeler, peel strands lengthways down the asparagus. Keep them in iced water until you are ready; this will make the asparagus curl which looks great on the plate.
- Now to construct the dish. Smear the whisked up grey meat evenly across the plate. Place the asparagus strands over the top. Next, carefully place the lobster over and around the asparagus. Lightly season the plate at this stage with a little salt and pepper and the remaining lemon juice. Lightly sprinkle over the dulse flakes, and then scatter the nasturtium, marigold leaves, fennel tops and flowers over the top.

BENDING *the* WILLOW

Weaving tender, flexible rods of freshly cut willow is a generations-old way of making containers for anything from sleeping babies to shopping. It's the traditional method in this part of the world for making the pots that catch crab and lobster too.

These days the pots are nearly all made of modern materials; more durable for sure but nowhere near as attractive to look at and, some would argue, a lot less friendly on the environment than the 100% biodegradable withy pots.

However, the art of making Cornish withy pots hasn't died out completely - fishermen Richard Ede from west Cornwall and Nigel Legge of Cadgwith Cove continue to make them and can both be found surrounded by people keen to see their skill in action at fish festivals and feast days around the county. Although Nigel uses the modern pots for his day-to-day fishing these days, he still gets sheer pleasure from shooting and lifting the occasional string of withy pots.

HOW A CRAB OR LOBSTER POT WORKS...

1 The pots are baited to attract the crabs or lobsters, then lowered to the sea bed on strings.

2 Markers depict each end of the string so the fishermen know where to find their pots.

3 The crabs and lobsters crawl into the pot through a funnel, either in the side or top of the pot.

4 Once through the funnel they enter the main chamber, known as the parlour, from where they are unable to find their way out again.

WITHY POTS

The same pots were used for both crab and lobster – with different baits to target one or the other.

Making and mending pots was one of the winter tasks for shellfishermen, who would typically have started their fishing season in the spring.

Like anything hand-made, each maker had their own little variations in style, which were passed down through families intuitively as the whole family mucked in to help.

The variations become greater over distance. Cornish pots, for example, tended to be made with an anti-clockwise spiral and straight, tall sides whereas the Devon tradition was for more sloping sides and a clockwise spiral.

HAVE A CRACK AT IT

The rusty-red of a freshly-cooked brown crab has, for many, always conjured up images of Cornish summer holidays, lazy lunches and salty sea air – but there's more to this much-loved crustacean than gilding fond memories.

JOFF LEE

LUXURY CRAB TART

This tart, devised by Rodda's, Cornwall's famous 125 year old dairy, is full of the flavours of the Cornish seaside. It makes an impressive lunch or, for a picnic or dinner party starter, try making 6 individual tarts.

INGREDIENTS Serves 6

375g pack ready-rolled short crust pastry (or make your own using 250g flour and 125g Cornish butter)

100g watercress, stems removed and leaves finely chopped

250g mixed Cornish crab meat

3 free range eggs

113g Cornish Clotted Cream

113g Cornish crème fraîche

¼ tsp dried chilli flakes

1 tbsp lemon juice

100g freshly grated Cornish extra mature cheddar

Cornish sea salt and black pepper

METHOD

● Preheat the oven to 200°C and very lightly grease a 22cm loose bottom flan tin. Place the tin onto a baking tray.

● Roll out the pastry until it's big enough to generously fit the tin. Ease the pastry into the tin, pressing into the edges and leaving excess pastry falling over the sides – don't trim at this stage. Prick the base with a fork.

● Line the pastry with greaseproof paper and fill with baking beans. Trim the excess pastry using a sharp knife. Bake the pastry case blind for about 15 minutes – remove the paper and beans and return to the oven for a further 10 minutes. Cool on a wire rack.

● Sprinkle the watercress on the bottom of the pastry case. Top with the crab meat, making sure it is evenly distributed.

● Whisk together the eggs and the clotted cream, crème fraîche, chilli flakes and lemon juice and half the cheese. Season well with the salt and pepper.

● Pour the egg mixture into the case. Sprinkle with the remaining cheese. Bake for 25-30 minutes, until the filling feels firm in the centre. Allow the tart to cool for 5 minutes before serving. It's great cold too.

CRAB BISQUE

Neil Haydock, The Beach Hut,
Watergate Bay

A warming winter soup flavoured with leftover crab shells – lovely served with crusty bread, a log fire and a stormy sea view.

INGREDIENTS Serves 4

2 x 450g Cornish brown crabs

200ml olive oil

2 medium-sized carrots, peeled

4 sticks celery

I large onion

2 cloves garlic

Small bunch of fresh tarragon

I heaped tbsp tomato purée

I tsp paprika

400g tinned chopped tomatoes

2 star anise

Good pinch of Cornish sea salt

500g cooked rice, rinsed well under cold running water

TO SERVE

Croutons or fresh bread

Spicy mayonnaise and Gruyere cheese (or try Cornish Kern as an alternative)

METHOD

- Heat the oven to 160°C. Next, prepare the crab. Crab bisque only uses the shells, so begin by picking out all the meat – this can be used separately for a salad, or is perfect for making the tart on page 43.

- Remove the crab gills (the grey, feather-like bits – sometimes known as Dead Men's Fingers), and dispose of them.

- Carefully smash the crab shells using a rolling pin – covering the shells with a tea towel while you do this will prevent too much mess. Take a large roasting tin and spread the pieces of broken shell across the bottom then drizzle with about half of the olive oil. Place in the oven and roast for 30 minutes, turning the shells occasionally.

- Meanwhile, finely chop all the fresh vegetables and the tarragon – using a blender achieves a finer, more uniform result.

- In a large pan add the remaining olive oil and sweat the chopped vegetables over a gentle heat for 10 minutes, giving them a stir every few minutes to prevent sticking.

- Next add the tomato purée and allow the mixture to cook for another 3 minutes before adding the roasted shells, paprika, tinned tomatoes, star anise and sea salt. Add enough water to cover all the ingredients. Bring the mixture to a gentle simmer for about 45 minutes, stirring now and then.

- Now add the cooked rice and blend all the ingredients with a hand blender – use a clean tea towel to cover the pan while you do so to avoid hot liquid splashing out.

- Finally, pass the soup through a sieve or conical strainer to remove the crab shell and the star anise.

- Check for seasoning and serve with a swirl of spicy mayonnaise and a sprinkling of grated cheese, alongside plenty of bread.

5 facts
you might not know
ABOUT CRABS

from Padstow
Seafood School

1 Think you've got the best moves on the dance floor?
You might have some competition with crabs who use their dancing skills to attract female partners by flapping their pincers and drumming their claws.

2 Wish you had eyes in the back of your head? Crabs have large compound eyes made up of over 8,000 tiny lenses, which means they can look in multiple directions at any time, including behind them.

3 Evidence shows that **humans have been eating crab since pre-historic times.**

4 62 different species of crab can be found around the UK; the smallest is the pea crab which only grows to a few millimetres.

5 Watching what you eat?
Crab meat is very high in vitamin B12, and the stomach-filling protein in crab will help you feel full for longer. It is also said to have anti-inflammatory properties and could help reduce blood pressure and protect against heart disease.

AROUND THE WORLD WITH CORNISH FISH

Rightly revered, there is little that beats the freshest fish, simply prepared. But with a greater variety of seafood landed at Cornish ports than anywhere else in Britain, making the most of Cornish fish and globetrotting flavour combos is half the fun for anyone with a serious sense of culinary adventure.

Cornwall's buzzing atmosphere, mellow climate and world-class ingredients (not to mention some of Europe's best surfing spots) make it a top settling spot for well-travelled, chefs and the diversity and hands-down freshness of the fish and shellfish is a big part of that draw.

Influenced by their experimental flair, the seafood scene has boomed with flavours and techniques that'll give you a round-the-world-ticket in a single mouthful.

The not-so-sleepy fishing port of Porthleven

used to be a well-kept secret among Cornish folk and holidaymakers in the know. In recent years it's become a hotbed of attention, thanks in part to some catastrophic storms, but also for its booming and varied food scene. Take a walk around the picturesque harbour and you'll find everything from soulful cafés to Bib Gourmand eateries, even Rick Stein's most westerly restaurant - all proudly flying the flag for the seafood that's landed there.

Arrive at the right time and you might even bag some freshly-caught fish and shellfish direct from the fishermen themselves.

EAST MEETS WEST

MONKFISH IS A FAVOURITE AMONG CHEFS FOR ITS ABILITY TO TAKE A LOT OF FLAVOUR, MAKING IT IDEAL FOR ADDING SOME SPICE TO YOUR LIFE AND EXTENDING THE BRIT-CURRY REPERTOIRE BEYOND THE USUAL INGREDIENTS. ONE OF THE SEABED'S MORE TERRIFYING-LOOKING DELICACIES, ITS APPEARANCE BELIES ITS VERSATILITY AND GORGEOUS MEATY TEXTURE, AND IT'S AVAILABLE ALL YEAR.

ROASTED MONKFISH WITH A SPICED LENTIL AND POTATO DHAL

Stew Eddy, The Square, Porthleven

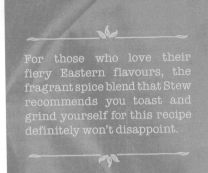

For those who love their fiery Eastern flavours, the fragrant spice blend that Stew recommends you toast and grind yourself for this recipe definitely won't disappoint.

INGREDIENTS Serves 4

4 monkfish portions (approx. 160g each)

2 tbsp vegetable oil

Bunch of coriander

Juice of 1 lime

Small pot of Cornish natural yogurt

DHAL SPICE

6 tsp cumin seeds

2 star anise

6 cardamom pods

1 cinnamon stick

2 tsp coriander seeds

½ tsp chilli flakes

½ tsp black peppercorns

4 cloves

DHAL

2 onions, finely diced

3 garlic cloves, peeled

25g fresh ginger, peeled

1 red chilli, deseeded

200g red lentils

2 tsp ground turmeric

Cornish sea salt

Splash of vegetable oil

POTATOES

2 waxy Cornish potatoes

2 tsp dhal spice

1 tsp turmeric

METHOD

- Preheat the oven to 180°C. Mix and toast the dhal spices on a tray in the oven for 3-5 minutes, then grind them to a powder.

- Dice the potatoes into small cubes, then add to a pan and just cover with water. Add 2 teaspoons of the spices and a pinch of salt, and bring to the boil. Cook until soft, and cool in the liquid.

- Wash the lentils, cover in plenty of cold water, bring to the boil and simmer for about 15 minutes until almost cooked.

- Meanwhile, for the dhal, grate together the garlic, ginger and chilli. Warm some vegetable oil in a pan, and add 8 teaspoons of the remaining dhal spices and the turmeric. Heat gently until the flavours are released. Add the garlicky mixture and cook for 30 seconds. Add the onions and slowly sweat down until soft.

- Drain the lentils and add to the dhal with some of the spicy potato water. Cook until the lentils are soft. Season to taste with Cornish sea salt, pepper and lime juice.

- Sear the seasoned monkfish portions in oil until golden, roast for 4-5 minutes, then remove from the oven and add chopped coriander, lime juice and salt. Rest for 2-3 minutes.

- Add the potatoes to the dhal and warm through, adding chopped coriander and lime juice to finish.

- Serve the dhal in bowls, place the monkfish on top and drizzle with natural yogurt and coriander (or micro coriander if you can get it). Stew's pineapple and lime pickle (see recipe on page 118) is the essential accompaniment.

SUSHI

SUPER-FRESH CORNISH FISH

Fish is the cornerstone of Japanese cuisine, but it has to be fresh and it has to be the best quality, especially for sushi and sashimi. If you don't like the thought of eating raw fish, it can always be cooked and marinated in teriyaki flavours, which work particularly well with Cornish sardines.

JAPANESE SHORT GRAIN RICE

Crucial for producing perfect sticky rice grains that will hold together.

KOMBU

Thick wide strips of dehydrated kelp that will impart some of that umami flavour to the rice as it cooks (you could use fresh foraged kelp).

JAPANESE RICE VINEGAR

For mild and mellow acidity.

CORNISH SEA SALT AND SUGAR

Essential for balancing the flavour of the rice.

A SUSHI MAT AND SOME NORI SHEETS

For making rolled sushi. Nori sheets have a textured side and a shiny side – the textured side sticks best to the ingredients it wraps around.

OTHER INGREDIENTS

Wasabi, pickled ginger, sesame seeds and pickled vegetables, for flavour, texture and colour.

Umami is a savoury taste described as the fifth basic taste sensation after sweet, sour, salty and bitter.

Sushi was one of the foods that chef Fiona Were hankered after when she arrived in Cornwall from her native New Zealand. In her home town, Christchurch, there is a significant Japanese population and the freshly made sushi, with its wasabi hit, umami rush and palate-cleansing pickled ginger, is exquisite, nutritious and affordable. Not so in Cornwall at that time, so Fiona decided that if she wanted to indulge her passion for sushi, she would have to make it. Unashamedly, she taught herself, and discovered a few simple tricks to guarantee that anyone else trying to recreate these delicious morsels of vinegared rice with an infinite selection of toppings and fillings will soon be hooked.

MAKING SUSHI RICE

GETTING THE RICE RIGHT IS FUNDAMENTAL TO SUCCESSFUL SUSHI

1. Measure out the amount of rice you need and use about 10% more water than the weight of rice. For example, 300g of rice will need 330ml of water. Wash the rice in a sieve until the water runs clear, then place in a heavy based saucepan. Add the water; it will just cover the rice. Place the pan over medium heat.

2. Once the water starts to simmer, place a square of Kombu on top of the rice (a 10cm square is about right for 300g rice). Put a lid on the pan and reduce the heat. Leave the rice to cook for 10 minutes, undisturbed.

3. Turn off the heat, remove the pan from the heat and leave the lid on. Set aside to rest for a further 10 minutes. Do not be tempted to take the lid off.

4. When this round of 10 minutes is up, remove the kombu from the cooked rice and spread the rice out in a tray to cool. There is no need to use any rice that is stubbornly stuck to the bottom of the saucepan.

5. Sprinkle over 2-4 tablespoons of rice vinegar and add salt and sugar to taste. If the fillings are strongly flavoured, the rice needs to be more salty and less sweet for balance. Carefully mix through the seasoning ingredients and then fan the rice to cool, gently turning it over at the same time with a spatula.

6. When the rice has cooled, it should be glossy. It is now ready to use but will keep for 12 hours in a cool place, covered with a clean, damp cloth. Never put it in the fridge; it will make the rice grains chalky and the result will be crumbly sushi that falls apart.

ROLLING SUSHI

Lift the end closest to you up, using the sushi mat to hold its shape.

Fold the roll and its filling over on itself, and gently roll it up.

When you get to the end, dab a small amount of water along the long edge, and seal. Use the sushi mat to gently roll back and forth until you have a tightly-sealed and compact roll, ready for slicing.

MAKING SUSHI

Fiona's Cornish sushi recipes include local substitutes for traditional Japanese ingredients, which she changes according to the season. Serve sushi with a dish of soy sauce for dipping, and choose your garnish to create a balance of flavours, textures and palate-cleansers. Try thinly sliced radish and gooseberry, pickled cucumber, or leaves and flowers of nasturtium. Sprinkle over some Sancho pepper for extra umami.

MONKFISH GUNGKO SUSHI WITH LEMON VERBENA

(Gungko means battleship in Japanese)

- Thinly dice 3-4 chunks of fresh monkfish, place in a bowl with a couple of dashes of yuzu juice and leave to steep for a few minutes. (Yuzu is a Japanese citrus fruit available in specialist shops. Use lemon juice as a substitute).
- Wet your hands in a water/rice vinegar mixture. Grab a small handful of rice and form into an egg shape.
- Wrap a 2cm nori strip around the long side of the rice ball (like the ribbon on a cake) and seal with a bit of sticky rice. Pat down the top of the rice ball.
- Dab with a tiny amount of wasabi, add a teaspoon of the fish and top with finely diced lemon verbena.

FISH 'N TIPS You don't need to use chopsticks to enjoy sushi. In fact, Nigiri sushi (handformed and topped with a generous slice of fish), the most popular type of sushi in Japan, is eaten with the fingers.

MONKFISH URAMAKI (California Roll) WITH NASTURTIUM

- Lay a sheet of clingfilm on the sushi mat, then a nori sheet on top, textured side up.
- Tightly press a thin layer of rice on top of the nori sheet, then gently flip the nori sheet over (so the rice is on the bottom).
- Add another thin layer of rice to the nori sheet.
- Chop some nasturtium leaves and layer on to the rice, followed by thin slices of red pepper and cucumber.
- Layer some monkfish (prepared as before) on top, along with a scattering of nigella seeds and some whole chives. Add a sprinkle of powdered dulse for flavour.
- Roll up gently and slice into 2cm segments.

CURED HAKE NIGIRI

- Steep 2-3 chunks of fresh Cornish hake in a mixture of soy sauce and black rice vinegar for an hour.
- Slice the hake lengthways through the middle, so you have thin strips.
- Wet your hands and form a small handful of cooked rice into an egg shape and dab wasabi on the top.
- Lay a piece of hake over the rice ball, and top with a bit of diced pickled ginger and finely chopped chives.

OYSTER NIGIRI

- Lay a shucked oyster gently on top instead of the hake.
- Top with a bit of finely diced pickled cucumber and apple, a thin slice of gooseberry and a sprinkle of finely sliced nasturtium leaf to finish.

TERIYAKI SARDINE ROLL

- Lightly poach 3-4 Cornish sardine fillets in a pan with soy sauce, honey and vinegar. Cool and set aside.
- Lay the nori sheet on the sushi mat, textured side up.
- Wet your hands and pat a layer of rice on to the nori sheet.
- Dab a thin line of wasabi onto the rice, and layer with thinly sliced cucumber and spring onion. Lay the sardine fillets on top, end to end, topping with some pickled ginger.
- Gently roll the sushi up and, using a sharp, wet knife, slice into 2cm segments.

If you become hooked on sushi, you may find yourself gathering all sorts of paraphernalia and ingredients along the way.

CORNISH BOUILLABAISSE

Will Gould, The Watch House, St Mawes

Originating in Marseille, Bouillabaisse was traditionally a handy way for local fishermen to use up the variety of smallfry that they couldn't sell. Will gives this rich, flavoursome fish stew a Westcountry twist by adding a dash of Tarquin's Cornish Pastis for a lovely liquorice undertone. You can play around with this recipe to your heart's content, but ideally your fish selection should include some of the chunkier fish such as gurnard, mullet, hake and some shellfish.

INGREDIENTS Serves 8

2 whole red mullet

2 whole red gurnard

1 small whole line-caught Cornish bass

200g hake fillet

200g monkfish

150g mussels

150g clams or cockles

1 spider crab, cooked and broken into pieces

50ml olive oil

2 onions, finely chopped

1 garlic bulb, cloves peeled and chopped

2 leeks, finely chopped

1 head of fennel, finely chopped (reserve the tops)

3 sprigs of fresh thyme

2 bay leaves

1 orange, zest off with a peeler and juiced

1 tsp fennel seeds

1 tsp smoked paprika

675g ripe vine tomatoes, chopped

1 tsp tomato purée

1 small bunch of flat leaf parsley, freshly chopped

500ml fish stock

1 tsp saffron stamens

500g small waxy Cornish potatoes, cooked

1-2 tsp Cornish sea salt

1 shot of Tarquin's Cornish Pastis

METHOD

- Descale and fillet each of your whole fish – or get your fishmonger to do it for you but ask for the heads and bones, which you will need. Chop all the fish into equal decent-sized chunks.

- Heat the olive oil in a large pan and add the onion, garlic, leek and fennel. Cook gently for 10 minutes, or until the vegetables are soft but not coloured, then increase the heat and add the fennel seeds, orange zest, paprika, thyme and bay leaves and fry for a minute to release the aromatics.

- Add the crab and fish trimmings and stir for 5 minutes before adding the orange juice, tomatoes, tomato purée and most of the chopped parsley, then the fish stock, saffron and 2 litres of water. Bring to the boil and simmer gently, uncovered, for 30-40 minutes, skimming the surface occasionally to remove any froth. When the broth has reduced to about 1.7 litres remove from the heat.

- Heat a clean pan on the stove and add the mussels, clams and pastis. Steam until the shellfish are open. Strain the seafood broth into the pan, add the potatoes and fish chunks and simmer until the fish is cooked and the potatoes are heated through.

- Use a slotted spoon to divide the seafood and potatoes into warm bowls and pour the soup over. Sprinkle with parsley and fennel tops and serve with garlic croutons and rouille (see page 118) or, for a simpler version, fresh crusty bread.

TASTE OF THE MED

We have a lot to thank the era of cheap flights for. It broadened our horizons and tickled our tastebuds with flavours from places with, it has to be said, more adventurous ways of cooking than the British Isles had mastered at the time. The countries around the Mediterranean, close enough for most people's budgets but far enough to be tantalizingly exotic, inspired modern British cooking more than any other, to the extent that we've made many of the ingredients and methods our own.

When it comes to bass, making sure you buy wild, Cornish and line-caught fish from a reputable source will help keep stocks healthy, and give you some of the best quality you'll ever taste. Cornish fishing has been a pioneer when it comes to improving the sustainability of wild bass stocks and implements no-net zones around the county's coast. Do your bit when buying bass and ask where your fish has come from and how it has been caught.

BASS NIÇOISE

Brian Johnston, C-Bay, Crantock

This recipe cleverly uses bass as an alternative to the classic tuna in a Niçoise style salad. Cornish earlies, in season from around June for just a short time each year, add another tasty Cornish dimension.

INGREDIENTS Serves 4

4 line-caught wild Cornish sea bass fillets

300g small Cornish early potatoes, scrubbed

100g asparagus, or fine green beans

3 free range eggs

200g fresh cherry tomatoes or 100g sundried tomatoes

25g fresh basil

Juice of ½ a lemon

2 tbsp balsamic vinegar

50g capers

75g black and green olives, pitted

1 garlic clove

4 tbsp olive oil

1 tbsp vegetable oil

Cornish sea salt

Bass has only recently become known as sea bass and the reason is a bit of a mystery – there aren't any freshwater bass in the UK.

METHOD

- Boil the eggs in salted water for 8 minutes. Drain and refresh the pan with cold water. Set aside.
- Make the dressing by blending together the garlic, olive oil, lemon juice and 1 tablespoon of the vinegar until smooth. Set aside.
- Cook the potatoes in boiling salted water for 15 minutes until a knife goes through easily. Drain and set aside.
- Cut the cooked potatoes in half. Heat up a non-stick frying pan and place the potatoes in the pan, cut side down, for 4-5 minutes until the cut side is golden brown. Toss the potatoes around the pan until they are browned all over.
- Put the tomatoes in a medium saucepan. Cook for 1-2 minutes on a medium heat until they start to blister. Add the potatoes to the pan and splash with the remaining vinegar. Stir in the olives and capers.
- Cook the asparagus or beans in boiling salted water for 4 minutes until tender. Drain.
- Remove the shells from the eggs and cut into quarters.
- Heat the vegetable oil in a large non-stick frying pan that has room for all the fish. Season the bass. Add to the pan and cook for 4 minutes, then turn over and don't touch for a further 4 minutes.
- Chop the basil and stir into the potato and tomato mix, which should be warm but not hot. Divide the mixture onto four plates. Add the eggs and the green vegetable and drizzle with the dressing. Place a bass fillet on top and serve straight away.

ALL ABOUT THAT BASE

No self-respecting Italian would top their pizza with anything other than the best fresh ingredients they could lay their hands on, and seafood is used much more extensively as a pizza topping in Italy than it is here. In fact, it's ideal as seafood loves the extra-hot extra-quick cooking treatment that a pizza needs to give it that essential crisp, slightly charred edge and a firm base.

WHEAL NEPTUNE

Jon Crwys-Williams, The Cornish Pizza Company, St Agnes

This decadent recipe created by pizza aficionado Jon takes pizza toppings to a whole new level with the luxurious flavours of fresh lobster and scallops.

INGREDIENTS

Makes two 30cm pizzas, each serving 1-2 people

DOUGH BASE

250g strong white flour, plus extra for rolling

1 tsp fresh or dried yeast

1 tsp salt

1 tsp olive oil

150g warm water

Semolina flour to dust worktops

NO COOK TOMATO SAUCE

400g can Italian tomatoes or 6 large ripe fresh tomatoes

2 tsp tomato purée

1 tsp oregano

1 tsp basil

Pinch of salt

Pinch of sugar

Pinch of chilli flakes

Pinch of ground black pepper

(Makes a jar that can be stored in the fridge for up to three days and can also be used as a base for a Bolognese sauce)

TOPPING

One medium Cornish lobster, cooked

6 hand dived Cornish scallops, cut in half lengthways

20 semi-sundried tomatoes

2 sprigs of fresh tarragon, leaves stripped and chopped

Juice of ½ a lemon

Cornish sea salt and freshly ground black pepper

Chilli oil

Street food isn't new to rural Cornwall.

The weekly fish and chip van has long been the only realistic hope that many villagers ever have of getting a take-away home while it's still hot. Jon and his wife Vicki have joined the burgeoning brigade who have taken to the road to expand the choice, popping up around the villages, campsites and festivals of Cornwall in their vintage VW camper complete with built-in pizza oven.

THE CORNISH PIZZA COMPANY

METHOD

- To make the base, place the dry ingredients in a bowl. Add the oil and warm water and mix to form a soft dough. Turn out the dough and knead on a floured board until it is smooth and elastic (10-12 minutes). Divide into two balls and pop them on a tray. Cover with a damp cloth or parchment and leave to rise for at least 1½ hours; ideally overnight. Once risen, you can store the dough in the fridge for up to 48 hours until you are ready to use it.

- To make the tomato sauce, place all the ingredients in a processor or blender and blend at high speed until smooth. Check the seasoning and adjust to taste.

- Remove the meat from the lobster (see method on page 35) and chop the tail meat into large pieces.

- Heat the oven to 220°C and preheat your baking trays or pizza stones.

- Dust the worktop with semolina flour then knead the risen dough balls lightly. If they have been chilled, allow them to reach room temperature to make them easier to work, before rolling out to form two 30cm rounds. You don't have to be too exact – a slightly irregular shape gives it charm.

- Dust the preheated baking trays or pizza stones with semolina flour then carefully place your pizzas on them. Working quickly, top each pizza with a layer of tomato sauce, spreading it right to the edges. Arrange the lobster, scallops and semi-sundried tomatoes evenly over the sauce. Season with salt and pepper and drizzle with chilli oil.

- Bake for 8-10 minutes, until crisp and golden.

- Sprinkle over the fresh tarragon and a squeeze of lemon juice and serve immediately.

FISH 'N TIPS To avoid a floppy bottom, your oven must be sizzling hot. A pizza stone can help but needs to be pre-heated for a good 45 minutes.

CULTURE SWAP

After the collapse of Cornwall's mining in the mid-19th Century, a quarter of a million people left Cornwall to try their luck in the New World. That's around half of the county's population today. Many ended up in Australia, where Cornish influences are still evident – with streets, villages and towns bearing Cornish names and adaptations of Cornwall's beloved pasty on sale. The exchange of cultures is more about the surfing than the mining these days, although the cooking comes into it too and Cornwall has benefited from some amazing cheffing talent from Down Under.

"look for wild, line-caught sea trout"

ALTHOUGH EXACTLY THE SAME SPECIES AS THE FRESHWATER BROWN TROUT, the sea trout makes its way to the ocean to mature. There its flesh takes on a pink colour due to its largely crustacean diet, making it easily confused with salmon – although it tastes completely different. To be sure you're making a sustainable choice, look for wild, line-caught sea trout and avoid the spawning season - from November to March inclusive.

Anyone who catches a sea trout needs a licence. If an angler or fisherman hooks one by accident without a licence, it must be returned to the sea alive.

WHO IS COUSIN JACK?
The nickname given to the Cornish miners overseas is said to stem from the way they greeted each other as 'cousin' and Jack being the most common name. A nicer tale is that it was because they were always asking for a job for their cousin Jack back home.

PAN-FRIED SESAME SEA TROUT

Bernie Powling, Godolphin Arms, Marazion

Bernie is the latest to swell the ranks of Aussie chefs on Cornish soil. He's added a hint of the Pacific Rim flavours prevalent in Australia to this dish, using distinctively nutty black sesame seeds.

INGREDIENTS Serves 4

2 x 200g fillets wild, line-caught sea trout, skinned

80g black sesame seeds

1 head of fennel, thickly sliced

400g fine green beans, trimmed

400g whole Cornish new potatoes, boiled

2 tbsp (or so) olive oil

3 oranges

60g maple syrup

Cos lettuce leaves

1 lemon, cut into 4 wedges

Handful of chopped parsley

METHOD

- First make the dressing. Peel the oranges and cut into cubes. Add a quarter of a cup of water to a pan, and add the orange cubes. Bring to boil and simmer until soft. Blend the oranges and the remaining liquid. Add the maple syrup and set aside to cool.

- Put the black sesame seeds in a bowl and use to coat each piece of fish. Set to one side.

- Heat a griddle pan until very hot. Drizzle with olive oil and add the fennel and green beans. Cook until grill marks appear, then transfer to an ovenproof dish along with the whole, cooked potatoes. Place in the oven at 180°C for 6 minutes.

- In a separate non-stick frying pan, add a splash of olive oil and fry off the coated sea trout for 3-4 minutes each side. Once cooked, remove from the heat, and take the vegetables out of the oven. Slice the potatoes (be careful not to burn your fingers) and get ready to plate up.

TO ASSEMBLE

Take four plates and add 2 leaves of cos to each. On each plate, gently layer fennel, potatoes and green beans then sprinkle with chopped parsley. Drizzle with the orange and maple dressing. Place a fillet of sea trout on top of the warm salad, add more dressing and garnish with a lemon wedge.

FISH 'N TIPS Cod or hake could be used as an alternative to sea trout.

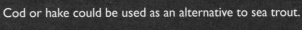

FOOD FOR THE SOUL

The hearty vegetable stews of southern Europe go really well with fish that have some character, and caponata, with its sharp hint of vinegar, is no exception. In its native Sicily, a dish like this might typically be served with red mullet, a fish that loves the warmer Mediterranean waters and gets both its stunning colour and rich, sweet flavour from the crustacea it lives on. The water around the Cornish coast is just warm enough to attract red mullet too – it's rarely found much further north.

MULLET WITH AUBERGINE AND BROWN SHRIMP CAPONATA AND ROCK SAMPHIRE

Chris Richards, Chris Smallwood and Matt Perry, The Queens Hotel, St Ives

When red mullet isn't around, this dish works well with grey mullet too, although the two are not directly related at all. It's thought the use of the same name was a mistake that simply stuck through common use. Grey mullet is much more like bass to look at. For good flavour, it needs to be fished in open water – if it's caught close to the shore it can taste muddy.

INGREDIENTS Serves 2

500g red mullet, filleted and pin-boned

1 aubergine

2 sticks of celery

1 red onion

4 plum tomatoes, quartered

1 garlic clove, finely sliced

½ tbsp caster sugar

Small handful of capers, plus some of the vinegar

90g fresh brown shrimps, peeled

Olive oil for roasting

Parsley and basil, finely chopped, to taste

2 handfuls of rock samphire

Vegetable oil for frying

Cornish sea salt and pepper

METHOD

- Preheat the oven to 160°C. Top and tail the aubergine, slice lengthways into four then chop into short chunks. Do the same with the celery.
- For the caponata - place the aubergine, onion, celery and garlic into a deep baking tray, drizzle with olive oil and mix, making sure every piece is well-coated. Roast for 20 minutes, then add the tomatoes, capers, caster sugar and caper vinegar, adding a touch more olive oil and tossing everything through. Return to the oven for 30-45 minutes (tossing another 2-3 times) until the tomatoes are soft and breaking down.
- When the caponata is ready, score the skin of the mullet fillets. Heat a non-stick pan with a small amount of vegetable oil and add the fillets, skin side down. Press gently down on the fish to ensure even cooking, turn the heat to moderate and cook for about 2 minutes.
- While your fish is cooking, add the chopped herbs and brown shrimps to the caponata and return to the oven to heat through.
- When the fish skin is cooked and crispy, flip it over. Slim fillets can come off the heat now but thicker fillets may need an extra splash of oil and an additional 1-2 minutes on the heat. Remove the fish from the pan and keep warm.
- Throw the samphire into the fish pan and return to the heat for about 30 seconds tossing constantly. You'll hear the samphire pop and crack as the small bulbs release their flavour.
- Present the fish fillets skin side up on a bed of caponata, garnishing with the samphire. This makes a light meal in itself or can be served with Cornish new potatoes and a seasonal green veg.

FISH 'N TIPS Think of rock samphire as the highbrow cousin of marsh samphire, though not quite as easy to find. It lives along clifftops and seawalls, sprouting from in between boulders – but never where it'll get its feet wet.

OUT & ABOUT

From dangling a hopeful rod over the edge of a harbour wall to twisting big, meaty mussels from the rocks as the low tide swirls around your ankles, the hunter-gatherer instinct means that, for many of us, the thrill of catching and cooking our own food is like no other. Getting your hands dirty every once in a while is medicine for the soul.

Cornwall's multi-hued coastline harbours a free and natural bounty – a dream come true for those who like to breathe in the fresh air, feel the sand between their toes and think outside the box when it comes to fixing a tasty morsel or two.

Good things come to those who know what to look for.

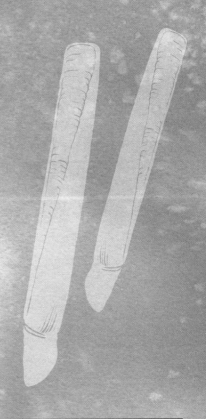

GONE TRIGGIN'

While there are few greater pleasures than a leisurely stroll along a Cornish beach, there's also a veritable larder that awaits you amongst the rocks and under the sand itself. Follow a few golden rules and you'll be happy as a clam…

ONLY COLLECT SHELLFISH WHEN THERE IS AN 'R' IN THE MONTH

During the summer months there is a bigger risk of algal blooms (which can make shellfish toxic) and a greater volume of bacteria in the sea, so the old saying does make sense.

SMART TIPS TO STAY SAFE
(and avoid food poisoning)

- Find out what you can about the water quality of coastal waters and estuaries from your local authority, the environment agency and local fishermen.
- Only collect shellfish from obviously clean areas. Find out where sewage outlets are and don't collect from harbours and marinas.
- Thoroughly cook all shellfish that you gather.
- Use the shellfish as soon as possible after gathering them.
- Make sure the shellfish are still alive before you cook them.

TOM YOUNG

MOTHER NATURE

Ecologist Caroline Davey is someone who knows her cockles from her clams and is Cornwall's go-to girl when it comes to anything handpicked, natural and oh-so-fresh. Running foraging courses from Fat Hen Cookery School's remote farmhouse spot not far from Penzance, Caroline is the master of letting nature's flavours do the talking.

TRIGGING is the Cornish word for collecting shellfish from the shoreline. 'Trigg meat' refers to what you gather.

RAZOR CLAMS

Meaty, sweet and very moreish, razor clams are the seashore's secret delicacy, surprisingly easy to collect but often overlooked. Caroline shares her tips to get razor clams above the ground and onto the plate.

YOU'LL NEED

A bucket

A tub of table salt

Sharp eyes and a bit of patience

CAROLINE DAVEY

HERE'S HOW IT'S DONE

1. Find the right kind of beach. A good start is to find a beach with razor clam shells on it, so you know they live there.

2. Look for the distinctive razor clam hole along the shoreline at low tide. It's not round but more like a keyhole.

3. Pour a bit of ordinary table salt down the hole and wait. If there's a razor clam in there the water in the hole will start to bubble and move about.

4. The razor clam will poke out of the sand – be patient and wait a little longer.

5. The razor clam will poke its head a bit further out, giving you enough of its body to grab and pull it out of the sand. Grab it before it changes its mind and goes back down into the hole.

6. They'll be quite happy kept cool and covered with seaweed in a bucket for up to 12 hours.

GRILLED RAZOR CLAMS

Caroline Davey, Fat Hen Cookery School

INGREDIENTS

Foraged razor clams (about 3-4 per person)

2-3 garlic cloves, chopped

1 red chilli, finely chopped

Zest of 1 lemon

1-2 tbsp parsley, chopped

Unsalted Cornish butter

METHOD

- Clean the razor clams and check they're alive by tapping them – they should snap shut. Discard any dead ones.

- Preheat your grill until it's as hot as possible.

- Lay the clams on a baking sheet and place under the grill until they open (1-2 minutes).

- Remove from the grill and set aside to cool.

- Pull the clams from the shell – rinse the shells and keep them to one side.

- Cut out the dark intestinal tract of the clam then cut off the round bulb-like end and the 'wing' covering the body. Finally, rinse off any sand still present on the clam to leave the white edible meat.

- Add the meat back into the cleaned clam shells and dot with butter, finely chopped garlic and chilli, lemon zest and parsley and briefly grill to reheat – ideally cook for no more than 3 minutes in total.

- Serve as a tasty light lunch or starter with fresh bread and a cherry tomato salad.

NET YOUR OWN

Is there a dish more reminiscent of simpler days gone by than fresh, buttery potted brown shrimps or British prawns with hot toast? Rolling up your trousers and spending a wholesome couple of hours with a net at low tide is one way of getting hold of these tasty crustacea.

It's easy to collect shrimps using a standard push net in the shallows at low water. They'll keep for several hours in a bucket of fresh seawater (around one hour if there's no water).

For prawns, you need a beach with large rocks, gullies and rockpools. Head there an hour before low tide. Push your net under the water, amongst the weed that grows in and around the rockier ledges (where prawns like to hide). Lift the net forward and up, bringing the prawns with you.

To prepare your foraged finds, just plunge into boiling water for a couple of minutes to cook then drain and cool quickly by plunging into ice cold water. Peel by removing the head and pinching the tail gently until the body pops out.

SHRIMPS VS PRAWNS
WHAT'S THE DIFFERENCE?

- Prawns hide in and around seaweed and rocky crevices — shrimps hide under the sand.

- A prawn's antennae are noticeably longer than a shrimp's — nearly double its body length.

- Shrimps swim; prawns walk.

POTTED SHRIMPS

Chloe Marsland, Harbour Lights, Coverack

Chloe's recipe, which gives this classic dish a flavoursome lift with smoked Cornish sea salt and a dash of spice, is a favourite at her beachside restaurant on the Lizard.

INGREDIENTS Serves 4-6

100g Cornish butter

450-500g fresh brown shrimps (peeled weight)

Zest and juice of ½ a lemon

¼ tsp mace

¼ tsp cayenne pepper

¼ tsp mixed spice

Pinch of grated nutmeg

Smoked Cornish sea salt and black pepper to taste

METHOD

- Melt 60g of the butter over medium heat; remove from the heat and leave to cool a little.
- Add the shrimps, spices and zest and juice of the lemon and season to taste (if you like spice then add a little more cayenne).
- Mix well to ensure all the spices are incorporated, and divide the mixture into small ramekins or Kilner jars.
- Melt the remaining butter over a low heat until it has clarified (when the white fats have separated from the clear yellow butter).
- Seal the top of each dish with a little clarified butter. and leave to set in the fridge for at least an hour.
- Serve with fresh sourdough toast and plenty of green salad.

FISH 'N TIPS If you're buying whole shrimps or prawns, you'll need about double the peeled weight.

PRAWNS

A bit like miniature lobsters, prawns have meaty flesh and make a tasty addition to a multitude of dishes. Not to be confused with their food-mile-heavy cousins from the Far East, prawns that venture close to the British shoreline are daintier - and many will say tastier.

They love the waters around Cornwall, which are that bit warmer than other coastal areas of Britain. The harbour of Mylor, near Falmouth, is known for its prawns.

MYLOR SHELLFISH COCKTAIL

Dale McIntosh,
Merchants Manor,
Falmouth

Head chef and hotel partner Dale eagerly awaits the short 6-8 week season for fresh Mylor prawns which starts around September.

INGREDIENTS Serves 4

400g very recently collected Mylor prawns, cooked

4 fresh native oysters

1 Cornish cock crab, cooked

100g sea lettuce

50g pepper dulse

½ small cucumber, peeled and diced into 1cm squares

3 free range egg yolks

Juice of ½ a lemon

300ml Cornish rapeseed oil

Cornish sea salt and black pepper

50g fresh dill

50ml white wine vinegar

2 tbsp caster sugar

Chefs often prefer cock crabs because they have larger claws than the hens and therefore more white meat.

METHOD

- Lay out the sea lettuce on a baking tray and place in a low oven to dry out. In the meantime, peel the prawns, leaving a couple with their shells on to garnish.

- Warm the sugar and white wine vinegar gently in a pan until dissolved, then add the cucumber and let the mixture cool – the cucumber will take on a sweet, pickled flavour.

- Meanwhile, shuck your oysters and set the juice aside, then put them into a food processor along with the lemon juice and egg yolks and blend. Whilst the machine is blending, add the oil in a slow trickle to thicken (like a mayonnaise), then add your oyster juice. Transfer the mixture to a jug or bowl and clean out the food processor.

- Break the claws off the crab and crack them open to extract the nice white meat inside. Pick through and season the meat with sea salt and pepper.

- Place the brown meat from inside the crab shell into the food processor. Add a pinch of sea salt and pepper and blitz for a good 5 minutes – this creates a smooth paste with bags of flavour and little effort.

- In a small deep fat fryer (or saucepan with 2cm of oil, heated to 120°C) carefully fry the pepper dulse in the rapeseed oil until crisp. Season and set aside.

- To serve, place the prawns on the centre of the plate. Using a palette knife, spread the oyster mayonnaise around the prawns, crumble the crab meat over the prawns, garnish with the oven dried sea lettuce and crispy pepper dulse and finish with the brown crab dressing.

ISLAND CATCH

Just 28 miles west of Land's End lie the Isles of Scilly, a magical little archipelago and a much-loved haunt for off-the-beaten-track holidaymakers. Distant enough from the mainland to have shaped its own character, it's still close enough for the 2,000 or so people who live on the five inhabited islands to feel connected to their Cornish cousins.

The Penders are one of the families whose names are implanted in generations of Scillonian history. They made Scilly their home at a time when subsistence living meant just that - farming and fishing to put food on the table. As tourism grew, so did the opportunities and fishing families like the Penders would sell some of their catch direct to restaurants and holidaymakers. However, the strong seasonal element to trade and the lack of anywhere or anyone to process the fresh fish meant that most of the catch from the islands' full time fishermen ended up back in Cornwall at Newlyn market.

Anyone caring to count the fish miles can work out the irony, and the cost, of Scillonian fish being taken to the mainland, while Scillonian restaurants and shops bought fish shipped across in the other direction. Until recently, that is, when a new generation of Penders, brother and sister Mark and Amanda, decided to take the plunge, quit their careers, and help their parents take a leap forward with a new way of doing things. Island Fish is the result.

Above: Granny Pender and her son Johnny picking crab

Working on the principle of selling everything within Scilly, the first step was to buy a second boat to increase the choice and volume of fish they have for sale. Next they created a small retail area at their home on the tiny island of Bryher, where they also pick the shellfish and clean and prepare the wet fish. By their own admission it's not rocket science but these two relatively straightforward steps mean it's now possible for islanders and visitors as well as hotels and restaurants to buy an attractive range of top quality seafood knowing that it's genuinely been landed on their doorstep.

"We are not selling fish, we are selling a story that is our heritage and love of Scilly. The future is as bright as we want to make it."

SPRATTING

IMAGES COURTESY AMANDA PENDER

One of the Pender family's traditions on Bryher is spratting - where everyone gathers on the shoreline to net the sprats that will come in on a big tide.

You can do the same on the mainland. Sometimes you can spot where the sprats are to be found by the number of mackerel about. The old adage about using a sprat to catch a mackerel is true – mackerel love sprats and will follow the shoals about. Seagulls love them too and will also signal when the sprats are close to the shore by diving for them.

ALL YOU NEED TO KNOW ABOUT SPRATS

- Cheap to buy and quick to prepare, it's worth looking out for these tiny fish when they're in season, even if you don't get a chance to go spratting yourself.

- They only make a mouthful each so you need at least 5 or 6 for each portion; more if you're hungry.

- Some people eat them whole - guts, heads and all – but if this isn't for you, simply remove the head and make a small cut in the belly and gut them under cold running water.

- Pat dry, season with salt and pepper and fry or grill quickly for 2-3 minutes each side.

- Serve with a wedge of lemon and a bowl of aioli for dipping (see recipe on page 118).

FISH 'N TIPS

Eating small, whole oily fish like sprats is very nutritious - the skin contains Omega-3 and the bones are a source of calcium. Oily fish also contain vitamin D, which the body needs to absorb calcium properly.

GOOD GRILLING

Fresh caught fish straight off the barbecue, with crispy charred skin and a hint of smoke, is the stuff of dreams. Turning those dreams into reality is pretty straightforward as long as you follow a few golden rules.

❶ To reduce sticking – the biggest challenge – always use a spotlessly clean, rust-free and well-oiled grill and get the coals really nice and hot before starting to cook.

❷ Whole oily or semi-oily fish such as Cornish sardines, mackerel, bass or bream, are best for the barbie. Their natural oils keep the flesh juicy and help prevent sticking. Simply scale, gut and clean the fish, place some fresh herbs and wedges of lemon in the cavity, season all over and pop on the grill.

❸ Fillets, cutlets and steaks of fish work OK as long as they're fairly chunky; about 25mm thickness is good. Thin pieces will break up or dry out and pieces that are too thick will burn on the outside before they're cooked all the way through. Always keep the skin on, to help hold the flesh together. Score the skin, oil the pieces all over, and try seasoning the cuts with herbs or a little spice.

❹ Cook swiftly over a high heat. Slow cooking will result in tough, dry flesh.

❺ Turn the fish just once, halfway through cooking. Don't be tempted to keep lifting it to check how it's getting on – fish can only take so much handling.

MONKFISH SKEWERS

For something a bit different, try a fish kebab. Monkfish is ideal because its firm flesh doesn't fall apart as it cooks, and marinating adds flavour and succulence.

A medium monkfish tail will make about six smallish skewers, which should feed two people.

METHOD

- Cut the monkfish tail into similar sized chunks and marinate for an hour or so. A simple mixture of fresh lemon juice and olive oil does the trick really well, or try combining yogurt, garlic, lemon juice and chilli.

- Thread the chunks onto the skewers, leaving a little gap between each piece. Any smaller bits should go at the end of the skewers so they can come off the heat while the others are still cooking if necessary. Add wedges of lemon to the end of the skewers if you like and then squeeze the roasted lemon juice over the finished kebabs.

- Turn the skewers as they cook to get that genuine chargill colour and flavour all over.

FISH 'N TIPS Avoid sugar or anything sweet like honey or orange juice in a barbecue marinade – it will just catch the flames and burn.

FIGURE OF 8 LOOP KNOT

Use to create a loop at the end of the fishing
line; handy for attaching weights or rigs.

BLOOD KNOT

Use this to join two lines together.

GRINNER KNOT

A knot to fasten hooks or swivels to the line, and the one
anglers like to use if they're aiming for bigger or weightier fish.

HOOK, LINE & SINKER

You don't need to be a seasoned salt-of-the-earth to appreciate the satisfaction of tucking in to a fish you've caught yourself just hours before. Stroll along any Cornish harbour and you'll see anglers from all walks of life lining the edges, keeping a weather eye out for that perfect catch.

Fancy joining them? It's easier than it might look…

ESSENTIAL KIT

Any tackle shop will advise, but these are the basics:

- A rod
- A reel and line
- Lead weights
- Hooks
- A brightly-coloured float

STAY SAFE

- Check weather and tide times before setting off.
- Always wear a lifejacket on open water or in exposed locations.
- Fishing off rocks is dangerous - the swell can pick up and sweep even the sturdiest angler off their feet and it's easy to get cut off by the tide.
- Keep an eye on children at all times.
- Tell someone where you are going and what time you expect to be home.

TAKING THE BAIT

Something needs to attract the fish to the hook by sight or smell. Bait therefore needs to be:

Wriggly - use live bait such as sand eels, lugworm and ragworm, or the rubbery and shiny imitations you can buy.

Pungent - try fresh or frozen mackerel, squid, sprats or octopus from tackle shops or the fishmonger.

Colourful - the bright colours in mackerel 'feathers' mimic the smaller fish that mackerel prey on.

FISH RESPONSIBLY

- Take only what you need.
- Know what you're catching – learn how to recognise different fish and avoid the spawning season.
- Stick strictly to the minimum catching sizes, which apply to anyone intending to keep the fish they catch, not just commercial fishermen.
- Take your paraphernalia home – stray fishing line is dangerous for all marine wildlife.
- Although stainless steel hooks look nice and shiny, they won't break down in the environment if you lose them, and can be damaging to wildlife. Use carbon steel ones instead.

FISH 'N TIPS

Fish tend to hide during the day and come out to feed when it's darker, so dawn and dusk are good times to try.

PLENTY MORE FISH

Doing things differently is an often endearing and sometimes bewildering Cornish trait. When it comes to measuring quantities of fish, there's no exception.

WARP [4 fish]

BURN [21 fish]

MEASE [505 herring]

CRAN [800 herring]

CORNISH HUNDRED [132 fish]

CORNISH LONG HUNDRED [8 times 120+5 fish]

CORNISH LAST [132,000 fish]

CORNISH OUNCE [16th part of a seine of fish]

TECHNIQUES

Fish is versatile and forgiving and lends itself to all sorts of preparation methods. In fact, the more you play around, the more addictive it becomes, and an armoury of skilful seafood techniques will set anyone up with oodles of inspiration for creating masterful dishes from scratch.

Surprisingly maybe, it's not difficult or complicated. These are skills that every family living around the coast would have known in the days when they had to make the best of whatever catch happened to be landed. Nowadays, many of the old techniques have been revived because they are such a good way of adding variety, flavour and texture to fish dishes.

HOLY SMOKES

Over the culinary course of time, fish has always been a prime target for debonair experimentation that can lead to some mighty fine flavours, and there's a revival going on among chefs for the ancient techniques of hot and cold-smoking. Freshly smoked fish have been on the hotlist of any restaurant menu worth its salt for years, but it doesn't get more wholesome than cutting out the middleman and smoking it in the comfort of your own kitchen. With the right pointers, it's simple and speedy too.

TYPES OF WOOD YOU CAN USE

(and the flavour intensity it produces)

Oak (strong)

Beech (moderate)

Ash (moderate)

Cherry (mild)

Apple (mild)

ADDITIONS TO YOUR CHIPPINGS

Tea leaves

Bay leaves

Rosemary

Thyme

Juniper berries

Lavender

CORNISH FISH FOR SMOKING

Sardines

Mackerel

Herring (for kippers)

Haddock

Scallops

Mussels

Oysters

HOT SMOKING
v
COLD SMOKING

Cold-smoking allows smoke to permeate the fish at room temperature without actually cooking it – giving a rich, strong flavour and colour.

Hot-smoked food is cooked in the heat of the smoke at around 70-80°C allowing the smoke to permeate as it cooks. Depending on the type of fish, it can be eaten immediately or enjoyed cold.

FISH 'N TIPS

Oily fish work much better than more delicate fish such as plaice or sole.

Fish has to be completely fresh to achieve the tastiest results – old fish will taste stale.

Shellfish like scallops or mussels respond really well to smoking, especially on a summer barbecue.

HOME SMOKED MACKEREL WITH CELERIAC REMOULADE AND PICKLED VEG

George Pascoe, Philleigh Way
Cookery School, Roseland Peninsula

TOBY LOWE

In this wholesome recipe, George puts a contemporary Cornish spin on the worldwide trend for this traditional preservation method – oak-smoking locally-landed fish using woodchips from trees grown metres from the Philleigh Way kitchen.

INGREDIENTS

4 tbsp Cornish sea salt

4 tbsp caster sugar

1 mackerel fillet per person, skin on and pin-boned

4 tbsp oak chippings

A sprig of rosemary

2 bay leaves

½ celeriac, grated

3-4 tbsp fresh mayonnaise

20 deep fried capers

12 ribbons of peeled carrot

12 ribbons of cucumber

Handful of pea shoots and fennel sprigs for decoration

PICKLING JUS

50ml each of water, white wine vinegar and white wine

50g caster sugar

1 banana shallot, diced

Chopped fennel and chives

YOU'LL NEED

Large frying pan with tight fitting lid

Trivet or wire rack to fit inside the pan

METHOD

- Heat all the pickling jus ingredients in a pan and pour over the carrot and cucumber. Set to one side.
- Cover the mackerel fillets with salt and sugar and leave for one hour to start the curing process.
- For the remoulade, finely grate the celeriac and mix in a bowl with seasoned mayonnaise.
- Line a large frying pan with tin foil and spread the oak chippings evenly over the bottom of the pan.
- Place a trivet in the pan. This will hold your fillets and suspend them over the chippings. (Alternatively place a cooling rack inside a roasting tin and wrap tightly with foil.)
- Rinse the fillets thoroughly and pat dry.
- Place the frying pan on a high heat and add the bay leaves and rosemary.
- When smoke starts to appear, lay the mackerel fillets (skin side down) across the trivet and place the lid on the pan.
- Turn down to a medium heat and let the fillets cook for about 5 minutes.
- Remove the lid and check the fillets, they should be slightly undercooked. Turn off the heat but put the lid back on and allow the residual heat from the pan to finish the fillets while they take on the smoky flavours.
- Lay your freshly smoked mackerel on a bed of remoulade, garnished with the rolled ribbons of pickled cucumber and carrot and finished with the capers, fennel sprigs and pea shoots.

THE CURE

ORIGINALLY A WAY OF PREPARING FOOD FOR PRESERVING BY REMOVING SOME OF ITS MOISTURE, A SWIFT AND LIGHT CURE IS A SIMPLE TECHNIQUE TO ADD A LITTLE FIRMNESS TO THE FLESH OF FISH.

SEAWEED CURED MACKEREL WITH HORSERADISH AND CUCUMBER

Tom Brown, Outlaw's at St Enodoc Hotel, Rock

Mackerel is one of the tastiest fish in the sea and it can sometimes be difficult to match all that flavour without overpowering it. This dish does the job skilfully, while balancing the natural oiliness of the fish perfectly.

INGREDIENTS Serves 4

MACKEREL

1 tbsp dried seaweed

4 large mackerel fillets, pin-boned

2 tbsp coarse Cornish sea salt

2 tbsp caster sugar

Cornish rapeseed oil

A few sprigs of dill

HORSERADISH YOGURT

200ml thick yogurt

3 tbsp creamed horseradish

Fine Cornish sea salt

CUCUMBER CHUTNEY

1 cucumber

½ green chilli, deseeded and finely chopped

2 shallots, peeled and finely chopped

2 cloves of garlic, peeled and finely chopped

50ml white wine vinegar

50g caster sugar

1 tsp yellow mustard seeds

METHOD

- To make the chutney, place a colander over a bowl and grate the cucumber into it, allowing the excess water to drain away. Place all the other ingredients into a pan and bring to the boil then leave to cool. Place the drained cucumber into a clean bowl, pour the cooled liquid over it and mix together.

- Place the yogurt and horseradish in a bowl and mix together. Pass through a sieve then season with salt to taste.

- To cure the mackerel, mix the salt and sugar together in a bowl. Lay the mackerel on a tray and sprinkle this mixture all over it. Cover and leave for 30 minutes. Wash the mackerel thoroughly in cold water and pat dry with kitchen towel then sprinkle it all over with the dried seaweed.

- Pre-heat your grill on the high setting. Drizzle a grill tray with oil and put the fish on it, skin side up. Place under the grill and cook for 2-3 minutes until the skin is blistering.

- Place each fillet on a plate and add a spoonful of the horseradish yogurt and a spoonful of the chutney. Finish with a few sprigs of dill and a drizzle of Cornish rapeseed oil.

RAW PASSION

Ceviche is a curing technique commonly used in Latin America, thought to have been introduced by Spanish conquistadors. Effectively, ultra-fresh raw fish is 'cooked' in the acidity of citrus juice, which denatures the proteins in the fish.

CEVICHE OF SEA BASS, APPLE AND VERBENA

Jack Stein, The Seafood Restaurant, Padstow

Middle son of Rick and Jill Stein and executive chef of the collection of Stein restaurants and the Seafood School, Jack is also a keen development chef, testing new recipes in the development kitchen. This one came about when Jack and his old friend Ross Geach from Padstow Kitchen Garden wanted to create a dish using ingredients from Ross's farm: bass landed at the bottom of his field, apples from his orchard and verbena leaves from his polytunnel.

It's perfect for a dinner party as all the preparation is done in advance to allow the sea bass to cure.

INGREDIENTS Serves 4

400g Cornish line-caught sea bass, filleted

½ crisp eating apple

100ml sunflower oil

20g verbena leaves

50g ponzu

Cornish sea salt

Chervil sprigs to garnish

METHOD

- Place the verbena leaves and sunflower oil in a food processor and blitz for 30 seconds until nicely broken up. Leave to infuse overnight and in the morning, pass through a sieve.

- Thinly slice the sea bass with your knife at a 45 degree angle as if slicing smoked salmon. Layer this on the plate slightly overlapping each piece.

- Add the ponzu to the verbena infused oil and stir gently to create a vinaigrette. Spoon over the sea bass until covered and add about 2g of sea salt. Leave to cure for 10 minutes.

- Thinly slice the apple, then julienne it into strips. Place 8-10 pieces on top of the sea bass. Garnish with a few springs of chervil and serve immediately.

FISH 'N TIPS Ponzu is a Japanese sauce available from specialist stores and online but 50ml each of lemon and lime juice works just as well.

PICKLED

A favourite in Nordic, Germanic and Slavic countries, pickling (also known as sousing when referring to fish) is normally associated with fish like herring and mackerel, where the acidity of the vinegar balances out their oiliness. Soused mackerel, made by marinating fillets of fresh mackerel in hot, spiced vinegar, then chilling them and serving cold, is a traditional family dish in Cornwall too.

RED WINE PICKLED SQUID

Ben Tunnicliffe, Sennen Cove

Ben's restaurant sits right on the seafront at Sennen Cove, where on a good day you can sit and watch the day boats coming into the harbour with their catch. One of Cornwall's original modern seafood pioneers, Ben shares his take on pickling; cooking fresh squid in a heady combination of vinegar, wine and spice. Squid can carry lots of flavour and is therefore ideal for this technique. The flavours will mature and soften with refrigeration.

INGREDIENTS Serves 2

1 medium-sized squid, prepped and cut into rings

450ml red wine vinegar

285ml red wine

3 shallots, finely sliced

12 fennel seeds, crushed

2 dried chillies

3 star anise

METHOD

- Place all the pickling ingredients in a saucepan, bring gently to the boil then add the squid.

- Cook – barely simmering – until the squid is tender (approximately 45 minutes).

- Leave to cool, then put into a sealable Kilner jar and store in the fridge for up to a week.

Serve this dish as a light lunch or starter with a dressed green salad and pickled cucumbers.

FISH 'N TIPS Squid will take either quick or slow cooking. Try it very lightly pan-fried with garlic, chilli and fresh herbs, or slow-braised with Deli Farm chorizo and finished with Cornish cream.

DIY SQUID

Squid is line-caught in Cornwall and is very versatile, but people are often put off buying it fresh for fear of knowing what to do with this odd-looking creature. Follow Ben's handy guide and you will never want to buy frozen, ready-prepared squid rings ever again.

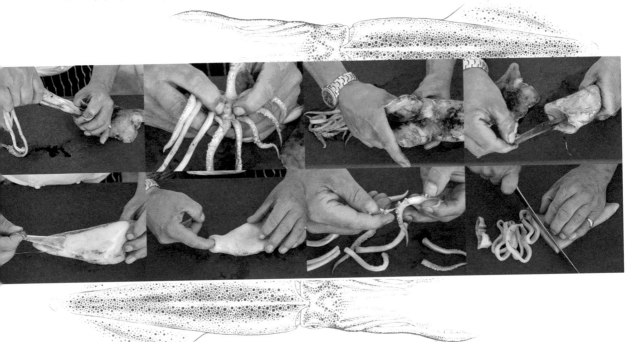

1 Hold the squid just below the eyes and pull the tentacles away from the main body.

2 Amongst the tentacles, you'll find a sharp beak – cut the tentacles off below the beak and put aside – discard the eyes, beak and innards from the main body.

3 Pull the 'wings' away from the main body and, laying them flat, cut away the tougher central section and discard.

4 Pull the 'quill' backbone out of the main body of the squid – it should come away easily as a long sheath.

5 Remove the darker coloured membrane from the surface of the wings and the main body with the flat side of a knife – it's quite sinewy and not pleasant to eat.

6 Turn the main body inside out by using your index finger (or the end of a wooden spoon) to push the narrower end inwards, then pulling it out the other side – this allows you to thoroughly clean the membrane and ink from the inside. Give the body a good rinse in clean, cold water.

7 Remove the membrane and tiny suckers from the tentacles – they'll pull off easily.

8 Slice the main body into rings around 1cm thick, and slice the wings into strips – the squid is now ready to use.

LIKE FATHER...

Sennen's harbourmaster and lifeboatman, Terry George, fished from the classically Cornish coves of Penberth and Sennen for almost 50 years, ever since leaving school. Even now, Terry still fishes commercially now and again, helping out his son Ben when times are busy, and launching the boats each day from the Sennen slipway.

Times have changed dramatically since Terry started fishing as a young boy and he treats technology with a level of scepticism – whilst webcams, echo-sounding and internet tracking may have their place, Terry credits his usefulness as a lifeboatman to the hundreds of hours he spent fishing the nooks and crannies of the Penwith peninsula, giving him a more intimate knowledge of the sea's hidden dangers than he claims any GPS could reveal.

He tells of times when fishermen would almost sink their boats, catching so much mackerel they would be knee-deep in it, sometimes only just making it to shore. Every fisherman these days seems to acknowledge those days are gone but you can guarantee that one thing hasn't changed – being 'top dog' is an accolade everyone still hankers after – and the nod of appreciation that's grudgingly given from all sides when you've landed the biggest catch is worth any number of eye-wateringly early mornings.

...LIKE SON

As one of Sennen's five full-time day boat fishermen, Ben George's life, like his father's before him, runs in synch with the weather and tides – venturing out almost every day to line-catch mackerel, pollack, bass, squid, and whatever else is in season. With a smaller fleet and much fewer fish around than just a few decades ago, the camaraderie is even stronger, the competition ever fiercer.

Having gone out with his dad since he was a nipper, the fishing bug has well and truly stuck – the freedom, the tranquillity of going solo, and the excitement of knowing every day will be different are part and parcel of a job that's never felt like a job, more a way of life.

Like many of the younger generation of fishermen, Ben has picked up on social media as a way of helping him stay connected to his friends and family, despite his lifestyle being anything but social. And at the click of a button, what might seem like just another dolphin pod or moody sunrise to Ben, allows those of us still under the covers at four in the morning to get a glimpse of a life totally removed from our every day.

The future isn't necessarily rosy though. Ben isn't sure if he would push his children into an unpredictable life of tide-watching, weather scares and those brutally early starts. But for him – he can't imagine doing anything else.

> "If it's in your blood, you can never get clear of it."

SENNEN COVE

THE SALT CRUST

Baking and roasting are great ways to cook whole fish and, if tackled correctly, the fish will come away from the bone easily but still be gorgeously moist. It's very tempting to overcook the fish this way, which leads to it falling apart. The solution: the salt crust. Encasing the fish with salt is a very simple way to keep all the flavour in and retain a firm texture at the same time.

SALT-BAKED RED GURNARD

Gurnard is a superb fish to cook with – and it's astonishing to think that at one time it was mainly used for pot bait. The absence of fishing quotas for gurnard has led to it being appreciated much more widely now, appearing regularly on fish counters and menus up and down the country. It's plentiful around the coast of Cornwall and definitely a fish to try if you're looking for something a bit different that you can buy with a clear conscience. It's also very versatile, makes a great goujon, but is just as tasty baked whole, following these few steps:

- Pop a few stalks of flat leaf parsley and thyme into the body cavity of whole, gutted and cleaned gurnard. One fish is about right for each person, but a large one will serve two.
- Sprinkle some ground sea salt all over the base of a roasting pan. Place the fish on top of the salt then sprinkle them with more salt, gradually building it up in layers to form a thick crust with no gaps anywhere.
- Bake for 25 minutes at 200°C. Don't be tempted to pick or prod the crust to see how it's doing.
- Remove the tray from the oven, allow to cool for a couple of minutes then gently tap the salt crust with the back of a spoon to crack it and peel it away from the fish.
- Remove the skin and carefully take the flesh off the bones. It's ready to serve how ever you fancy – a heap of fresh salad leaves or a pile of chips will be equally good.

BETTER BATTER

The secret of deep-fried fish is really crisp, light batter – and it's harder than you think. However, help is at hand with this extra-easy trick of using gluten-free self-raising flour. The Xanthan gum and bicarbonate of soda in it react under heat to produce more bubbles and therefore a crispier result, midway between a tempura and a classic British batter.

SHARP'S ATLANTIC BATTERED COD CHEEKS

Zack Hawke, The Mariner's, Rock

Using beer in batter adds body, lightness, colour and flavour. Zack uses Sharp's Atlantic ale pulled straight from the cask at The Mariners and adds sparkling water for extra bubbles because the ale isn't carbonated. If you use the bottled version you'll have enough bubbles with the beer alone.

INGREDIENTS Serves 3-4

1.5 litres Cornish rapeseed oil

Enough ice to sit the batter over

12 cod cheeks, sinew removed (ask your fishmonger)

Gluten-free flour for dusting the fish

Cornish sea salt flakes

FOR THE BATTER

250g gluten-free self-raising flour

400ml Sharp's Atlantic Ale

METHOD

- Place the oil in a deep fat fryer or deep heavy pan and pre-heat to 185°C.
- Whisk together the gluten-free flour and beer. Sit it in a bowl over the ice and leave for 5 minutes to start activating.
- Dust the cod cheeks in the extra gluten free flour. Dip the cod cheeks in the batter, shake off any excess. Place carefully in the fryer, dropping the fish away from your body to avoid splashing any hot oil on yourself. Don't overcrowd the fryer as this will reduce the temperature of the oil and also increase the risk of the cheeks sticking together.
- Fry for 3-4 minutes until crispy and golden. Lift out of the fryer with the slotted spoon, straight onto kitchen paper. Drain for a minute then season with Cornish sea salt flakes.
- These are wonderful served with garlic and lime mayonnaise (there's a great recipe in Nathan Outlaw's Fish Kitchen book) and a wedge of lime.

 FISH 'N TIPS   Monkfish cheeks are a great alternative for this dish.

Cod cheeks are a part of the fish that would normally be discarded or used for stock. They are delicious, with quite a sweet flavour and have become more popular recently as interest has grown in sustainability and using as much of the fish as possible - in the same way as nose to tail eating came around with meat a few years back. As they are still regarded as a by-product you can pick them up relatively cheaply from a good fishmonger.

MEGRIM WITH NETTLE PASTA AND ROCK SAMPHIRE

Mark Devonshire

Megrim may not be much to look at but it tastes beautiful. It's landed in abundance in Cornwall and is very good value, but rarely used in Britain. Who knows why? Private chef, teacher and events caterer Mark is on a mission to set that right. Here he pairs the megrim with an unusual, delicate nettle pasta. Before you start, head out into the garden or a leafy lane and carefully pick a good selection of young nettle leaves. Use gloves and pick the top 4 leaves, which are soft and tender.

INGREDIENTS Serves 2

1 whole large megrim, filleted

100g seasoned flour

50g unsalted Cornish butter

1 tsp toasted fennel seeds

Wild mallow flowers

50g parmesan cheese

Splash of olive oil

SAUCE

175ml dry white wine

140ml fish stock

140ml Cornish double cream

80g unsalted Cornish butter

Bunch of rock samphire

Juice of a small lemon

Cornish sea salt and black pepper

PASTA

200g Italian '00' flour

2 medium free range eggs (1 whole and 1 yolk)

100g fresh nettles

Semolina flour for dusting

METHOD

- Cook the nettles in a pan of boiling water for 30 seconds. Remove with a slotted spoon, place on a tea towel, gather them into a pile and gently squeeze the water out. Blend in a food processor.

- Add the pasta flour to the food processor and pulse it. Add the whole egg and egg yolk and keep running until the mixture forms a ball. If the dough is too wet, add more flour. Tip out the dough, knead until smooth, wrap in cling film and leave to rest in a cool place for 1 hour.

- Pass the dough through the pasta machine with the rollers at the widest setting. Repeat this process, folding between each pass, until the dough becomes elastic.

- Now stretch the pasta by decreasing the roller setting with each pass, without folding the pasta between passes. Once you have reached the final setting, lay the length of pasta on a work surface dusted with semolina flour. Leave to dry for about 20 minutes.

- With the tagliatelle cutters on the machine, introduce the dough while gently turning the wheel. Now your pasta is ready to cook. Bring a large pan of salted water to the boil, ready to pop the pasta in just before serving.

- For the sauce, place the stock and white wine in a pan, bring to the boil and simmer until reduced by half. Add the cream and reduce again gently to a sauce consistency. Beat in the butter, making the sauce smooth and shiny. Stir through the samphire with a good squeeze of lemon juice and season to taste. Keep warm on a gentle heat.

- Lightly cover the megrim fillets with the seasoned flour. Melt the butter in a large frying pan, add the fish in a single layer and cook on a medium high heat for about 2 minutes each side until the fillets have turned lightly golden.

- While the fish are cooking, boil the pasta for no longer than 2-3 minutes, drain into a colander and drizzle with olive oil to prevent it from sticking together.

- Pile the pasta into warm bowls. Pour the sauce over and lay the fish on the top (pouring the sauce over the fish will make it soggy). Garnish with toasted fennel seeds, wild mallow flowers and freshly grated parmesan.

PERFECT PASTA

Pasta and seafood aren't always obvious bedfellows but the right combination makes magical eating. The trick is to use fresh pasta, the art of which is easier than you might think. Once you've learnt the technique you'll be hooked and can play around with recipes to your heart's content.

Patience pays off. It might take as many as 20 passes to get the pasta sufficiently smooth and elastic before you start decreasing the setting on the machine, but the result will be worth it.

—UP YOUR—
GAME

Many people say they would cook more with seafood if they felt more confident handling it. We challenged accomplished seafood chef **Paul Ripley** to answer some of the more pressing FAQs...

Q: What are the key ingredients you'd never be without when cooking fish?

A: Simplicity is everything and you won't go far wrong with garlic, olive oil, sea salt, fresh herbs and lemon. It's always good to have some good fish stock at hand too – keep some in the freezer.

Q: What type of sauce goes with different types of fish?

A: The key is balance. A classic wine and cream sauce will lift a low-fat white fish, whereas oily fish work well with something acidic. Gooseberry sauce with mackerel might sound like an odd combination but the two complement each other perfectly.

Q: Is it better to cook fillets or whole fish?

A: Fillets are easy and a whole fish doesn't suit all recipes, so ring the changes. A steak cut through the fish, which you can do with hake, turbot and other larger fish, will mean that the flesh is cooked on the bone and you will get that wonderful extra juiciness and flavour.

Q: Do I have to scale fish?

A: Scaling whole fish is a necessary chore as the scales aren't pleasant to eat. Any fishmonger will be happy to do it for you but it's an easy technique to master at home. Removing scales can be a messy business though, so put the fish into a plastic bag to catch the blighters!

Q: Am I meant to eat the skin of fish?

A: All skin is edible but some is tastier than others. The skin of oilier fish crisps up really well and in many countries is regarded as a delicacy in its own right as it can take on the flavour and aromas of pork crackling. The skin of the bream family is especially good.

Q: Is frozen fish inferior to fresh fish?

A: The thing about fresh fish is that it's much easier to find out where it's come from and how it's been caught, plus you can check the quality for yourself. Fillets of most fresh fish will retain their quality for up to two months in the freezer if well-wrapped.

Q: What's the correct thing to do with all the accompaniments that are served with classic fish soups and bisques?

A: The rouille is spread onto your garlic croutons, usually topped with grated parmesan cheese and floated on the soup. The heat of the soup will soften the crouton and the rouille and cheese will fall into the soup allowing you to stir it in slightly. Delicious!

Q: What's a good trick to add flavour to fish?

A: Fish cooks pretty quickly; if you're cooking it in water, add the flavours to the water so they impregnate the fish while it's cooking. This is known as a court bouillon which many recipes call for. Wine, vinegar and lemon juice are the classics.

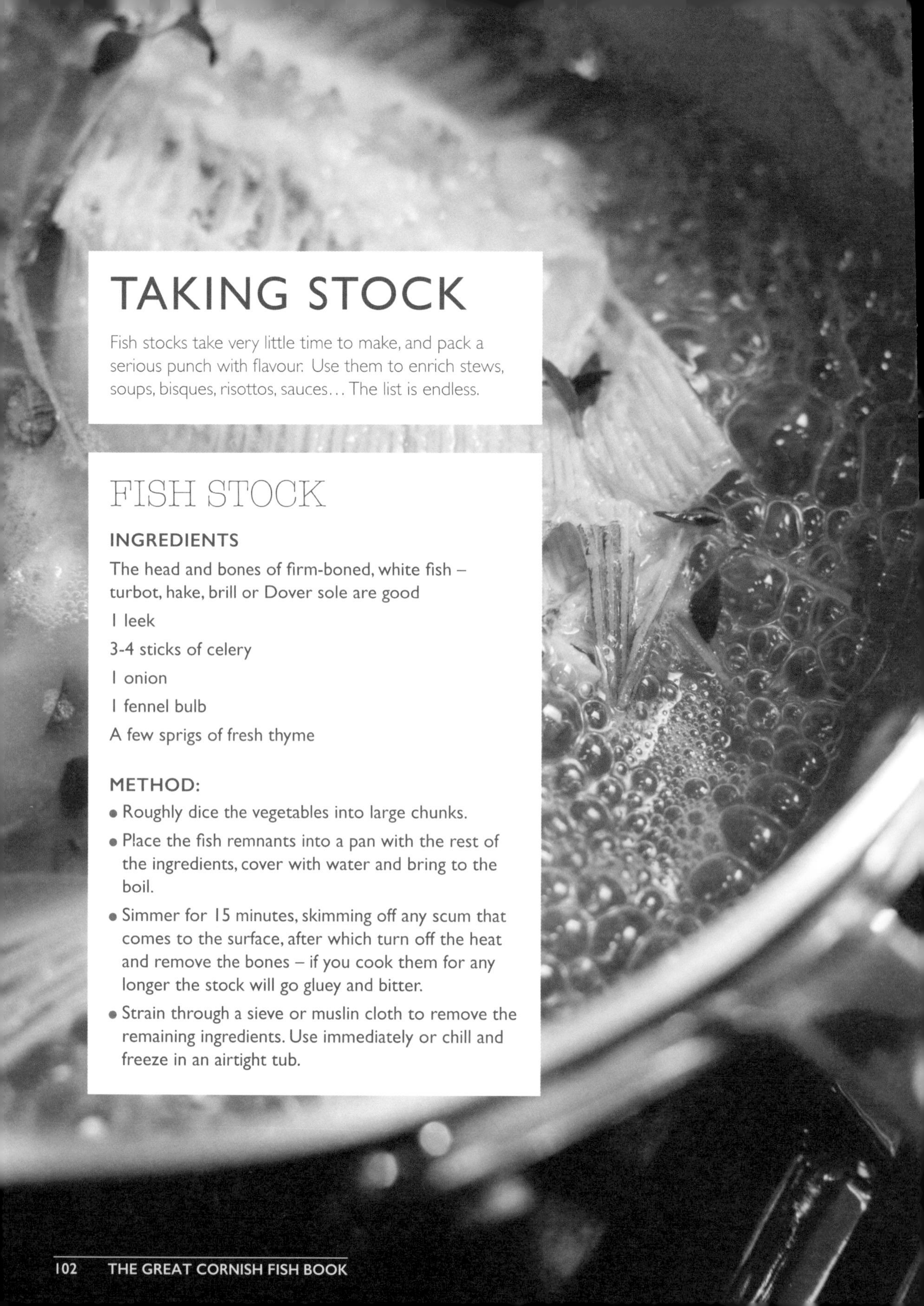

TAKING STOCK

Fish stocks take very little time to make, and pack a serious punch with flavour. Use them to enrich stews, soups, bisques, risottos, sauces… The list is endless.

FISH STOCK

INGREDIENTS

The head and bones of firm-boned, white fish – turbot, hake, brill or Dover sole are good

1 leek

3-4 sticks of celery

1 onion

1 fennel bulb

A few sprigs of fresh thyme

METHOD:

- Roughly dice the vegetables into large chunks.
- Place the fish remnants into a pan with the rest of the ingredients, cover with water and bring to the boil.
- Simmer for 15 minutes, skimming off any scum that comes to the surface, after which turn off the heat and remove the bones – if you cook them for any longer the stock will go gluey and bitter.
- Strain through a sieve or muslin cloth to remove the remaining ingredients. Use immediately or chill and freeze in an airtight tub.

SHELLFISH STOCK

INGREDIENTS

The picked-over shells of 1-2 cooked crabs or lobsters

Cornish butter or rapeseed oil

1 onion

1-2 sticks of celery

1-2 carrots

1 can of chopped tomatoes

2 garlic cloves, crushed

2 bay leaves

1 tbsp black peppercorns

A few sprigs of fresh thyme

Cornish sea salt, to taste

METHOD:

- Roughly dice the onions, celery and carrots.
- Preheat the oven to 200°C. Place the picked-over shells in a roasting tin and roast for 15-20 minutes, turning once or twice. Remove from the oven and crush the shells roughly with a rolling pin or mallet.
- Meanwhile, melt the butter in a large frying pan and sweat the onions, celery and carrots on a medium heat for 5 minutes.
- Add the herbs, seasoning, garlic and the newly roasted shells, give it a good stir and then add the tinned tomatoes.
- Top up with around 1.5 litres of water and bring to the boil, then reduce to a simmer and keep on the hob for about 20 minutes.
- Strain through a sieve or muslin cloth to remove the shell and other bits. Use immediately or chill and freeze in an airtight tub.

FISH 'N TIPS

Roasting the shells before you make the stock will intensify all those lovely flavours.

Picked shells and leftover fish bones can be stored in the freezer until you've got enough (or enough time!) to make a stock with them.

AQUA-CULTURE

Fishing is the last true form of hunting that we rely on for food and we've only relatively recently begun taking fish out of the wild and farming them.

One type of aquaculture that isn't so new is shellfish farming. In fact, oyster farming dates back to the Romans, who it's thought introduced Britain to the whole concept of eating shellfish as a delicacy. Shellfish farming has come and gone in the intervening centuries but nowadays there is a massive revival as thoughts turn to the ability of self-sustaining, readily-breeding and nutrient-packed molluscs like oysters and mussels to help feed a growing global population.

Around the Cornish coasts today, aquaculture is focussed on the low intervention and low impact production of shellfish. Sensitively done, it's standing the test of time, providing a high quality food source while enhancing - rather than ransacking - the natural environment.

OYSTER FARMING

Ostrea edulis, known as the common or native oyster, has been around on the planet for millions of years, longer in fact than humans. A simple, bivalve mollusc, it can live for up to 15 years and feeds by filtering nutrients from the seawater that passes through its system.

Oysters have only relatively recently taken on their association with the Champagne set. For generations they were a cheap form of mineral-rich protein for ordinary folk. At their peak in the mid-1800s, it's thought that around 500 million native oysters were harvested in one year in Britain, a far cry from the 25 million that were being produced when brothers-in-law Ben Wright and Robin Hancock took on the lease of the derelict Duchy Oyster Farm on the Helford River in 2005.

Their aim was to help reinvent attitudes to the oyster in this country; in particular, to remove its exclusivity and get more people enjoying oysters, trying different varieties and distinguishing the flavours that come from cultivating them in habitats with differing levels of minerality. To overcome the seasonality of the native species, they decided to cultivate the hardier Pacific oysters too, taking care to use only non-spawning stock to protect the balance of the indigenous eco-system.

Ten years on, their certified organic oysters can be found not only at their pub The Ferryboat Inn on the banks of the Helford, but in their three London oyster bars and many other London restaurants too.

By resurrecting the oyster farm and introducing large numbers of these natural filter-feeders, the water quality has improved greatly too, increasing the bio-diversity of the river and proving that aquaculture can have a positive impact on ecosystems.

WHAT DOES AN OYSTER TASTE LIKE?

"Absolutely unique, eating a fresh raw oyster is like kissing the ocean"

DOING YOU GOOD

Laden with minerals, rich in protein, but virtually fat-free, an oyster is one of the earth's natural superfoods.

HOW DO YOU EAT YOURS?

NAKED
Max the natural flavour

A SQUEEZE OF LEMON
Gently highlight the taste of the ocean

A DASH OF TABASCO
For oysters that kick

SHALLOT VINEGAR
Add complexity

HOW TO GROW AN OYSTER

This is how it's done at the Duchy Oyster Farm:

The tiny seed (baby) oysters are bought in when they are either 2mm or 7mm and placed in a poche (a tightly meshed bag).

The poches are placed in cages that sit on the bottom of the river.

To provide enough room for growth, they are monitored and gradually divided.

When they are able to fend for themselves they are taken to Frenchman's Creek to mature at low densities.

Once harvested, they go through a purification process using UV light, before being sold.

No chemicals or artificial processes are used at any stage.

SMOKED OYSTERS WITH BEETROOT AND CRÈME FRAÎCHE

Robert Bunny, The Ferryboat Inn, Helford Passage

For those who can't get to grips with oysters in the raw, this recipe using them lightly smoked is ideal and makes a simple but impressive lunch. Bunny – as he's affectionately known – uses a stove-top smoker but you can follow the instructions on page 83 for an alternative method for the smoking part of the recipe.

INGREDIENTS Serves 4

12 Cornish oysters

1 medium uncooked red beetroot, peeled

1 tbsp white wine vinegar

1 tsp Dijon mustard

1 tsp caster sugar

Pinch of fresh dill, chopped

100g Cornish crème fraîche

1 tsp horseradish sauce

Cornish sea salt and pepper

METHOD

- Grate the raw beetroot into a bowl and add the vinegar, mustard, sugar and dill. Season with sea salt and pepper and mix thoroughly. Set aside to let the flavours mingle.

- Place some beech chips in a stove-top smoker, put the lid on and warm it until there is heat and smoke in the box.

- Shuck the oysters and strain off any excess liquid. Place the oysters on a rack and put in the smoker on a medium heat for 5 minutes or until the oysters are warm and slightly firm. Do not overcook or allow the smoker to get too hot, as the oysters will harden.

- Put the crème fraîche into a bowl, add the horseradish, then season to taste and mix well.

- To serve, place the oysters on a serving plate, with a spoonful each of the crème fraîche mixture and pickled beetroot and a couple of slices of good bread.

Mussel Farming

Mussels have been cultivated in Europe for generations, but out in St Austell Bay a new type of mussel farm has arrived. Fed up with water quality problems in the estuaries, where mussels are traditionally cultivated, Gary Rawle shifted his Westcountry Mussels business into open water in 2011. Hardly visible from the shore, the farm covers an area the size of 20 football pitches.

Making a huge investment, involving 200 tonnes of anchors and 70 miles of rope, was quite a risk, especially when a lot of the local fishermen who knew the bay warned him that the farm wouldn't survive bad storms. But Gary's 'nothing ventured, nothing gained' philosophy paid off. The mussels he harvests now grow to the same size in 15 months as those he was farming in the estuaries reached in 2½ - 3 years and, with a meat to shell ratio of 60%, he reckons his are some of the best anywhere.

Echoing the thoughts of the oyster farm, he feels his methods are adding something to the ecosystem rather than taking anything away. The mussels grow completely naturally; there is no by-product or discard; the water is clean; and other marine creatures that love mussels, such as lobsters, are attracted by the ones that get away and fall to the seabed.

The downside? Being out in open water means more days are lost due to bad weather and, for a man who gets sick on a puddle, working on a rolling deck isn't a natural choice.

FISH 'N TIPS GARY'S TIP – It's not necessarily true that if a mussel is open before you cook it, it means it is dead and should be discarded. A much better test is to tap the mussel on a hard surface – if it's alive it will move. If it doesn't move, don't use it.

CAMEL VALLEY MUSSELS WITH TARRAGON, SHALLOTS & GARLIC

Lee Trigger. The Park Café, Mawgan Porth

INGREDIENTS Serves 2

1kg fresh mussels

1 shallot

2 cloves of garlic

50ml Camel Valley Brut

1 tbsp fresh tarragon

200ml Cornish double cream

METHOD

- Remove the mussel beards under cold running water, then scrape away any barnacles with the back of a knife.
- Chop the shallots and garlic finely and roughly chop the tarragon.
- Heat a large saucepan with a tightly fitting lid.
- Throw all the ingredients apart from the cream into the hot dry saucepan, replacing the lid so the steam does not escape.
- As soon as the mussels begin to open, add the cream and replace the lid.
- When the liquid returns to the boil and rises to immerse the mussels, remove the lid for a minute or two and then serve immediately.
- Remember to discard any unopened mussels and serve with a good quality fresh bread and Cornish butter.

 FISH 'N TIPS Don't be tempted to stir or shake the mussels too much – this will make them fall out of their shells.

MUSSEL BEARDS

These are the tough threads that attach the mussel to rocks in the wild. Just before cooking, remove the beard by pulling it out sharply at the root – it can be very strong so use pliers for extra leverage.

 It's certainly true that the better the wine you cook with, the better the result will be. A snifter of Camel Valley's famous fizz gives a lovely, buttery overtone to this dish, and there'll be plenty left in the bottle to make a rather decadent meal of it as you eat (or as you cook if you can't wait). The vineyard's Atlantic Dry is a seafood-friendly alternative.

A PERFECT MATCH

A silky-soft sauce with a tang of garlic. A crisp, cold, aromatic beer. A fantastic meal is about much more than the dish on the plate. Sometimes, it's the accompaniments that make a dish exceptional, and every cook knows that good flavour loves good flavour.

Salt n' vinegar, we salute you! But reach out of that comfort zone and you'll find a wealth of possibilities to give a final flourish to your fish. Quick to prepare, with just a few ingredients, discover perfect partners for a whole variety of seafood dishes, from the conventional to the avant-garde.

The drinks options are plentiful too and the spectrum for seafood matches that make the tastebuds dance is delightfully wide. Whether it's wine, beer, cider or spirit, the right drink can lift and enhance the qualities of a perfectly cooked crab, a freshly griddled sardine or a fragrant seafood curry, to name just a few.

We'll drink to that…

QUICK TARTARE SAUCE

A must for dipping white fish goujons.

Finely dice 2-4 pickled gherkins and a handful of capers. Add them to a bowl of good-quality mayonnaise with a squeeze of lemon juice and mix thoroughly. Season with sea salt and freshly ground black pepper to taste.

QUICK TOMATO SAUCE

The real chip-dipping deal. Try this speedy idea from the Cornish Ketchup Company.

Bring all these ingredients to the boil in a medium size pan: 500g cored and chopped ripe vine tomatoes, 50ml cider vinegar, 2 tablespoons each of Worcester sauce and brown sugar, ½ teaspoon each of onion granules, garlic granules, paprika and sea salt. Boil rapidly for 10 minutes or until it starts to get sticky. Remove from the heat and blend in a food processor. Pass through a sieve and leave to cool. Store in an air tight container in the fridge for 2-3 weeks.

ROUILLE

A must for fish stews and soups. This is Will Gould's recipe.

In a food processor, thoroughly blend 1 cooked and peeled potato, 4 egg yolks, 3 crushed cloves of garlic (plus an optional handful of wild garlic), a pinch each of paprika and cayenne pepper, the juice of ½ a lemon and a teaspoon of hot water. Then with the motor running, slowly drizzle in 250ml of light olive oil to emulsify.

AÏOLI

Gorgeous garlic mayonnaise with myriad uses. Try it alongside barbecued fish.

Whizz 2 cloves of garlic with 1 teaspoon of Dijon mustard and 2 free range egg yolks in a blender. With the motor running, slowly stream in 275-300ml of Cornish rapeseed oil until smooth and thick. Finish with a good squeeze of lemon or lime juice and Cornish sea salt, then chill for 30 minutes to let the flavours develop.

PINEAPPLE AND LIME PICKLE

Stew Eddy's fresh and zesty pickle gives zing to earthy fish curries. This makes 4-5 small jars and will keep in the fridge for a couple of weeks.

Peel the green skin from 4 limes and cut it into strips, then blanch in boiling water until soft. Halve and juice the limes. Sweat a sliced onion in oil until soft, then add chopped garlic, chilli and ginger to taste, along with the lime zest, 4 teaspoons of dhal spice (see recipe on page 49), 1 teaspoon of turmeric and 2 teaspoons of Madras curry powder. Cook for 2 minutes, add 4 teaspoons of tomato paste and cook for another minute, then stir in 200g each of raisins and demerara sugar plus 200ml of white wine vinegar. Simmer slowly for around 30 minutes until syrupy then pour into sterilised jars.

BLUESAIL FISH

LOOE HARBOUR 2011

COVERACK

BLUESAIL FISH

LOOE HARBOUR 2011

LOOE HARBOUR 2011

BLUESAIL FISH

LOOE HARBOUR 2011

LOOE HARBOUR 2011

COME FRY WITH ME

Few summers are complete without perching on the edge of a harbour wall or clifftop bench, dodging seagulls and munching your way through a paper-wrapped portion of crisp, deep-fried fish with golden, finger-lickingly-salty chips.

When it comes to recreating that classic partnership, the heavenly results you'll get from frying your own fresh potatoes will be infinitely tastier than anything you'll find in the freezer. Frying is a great way of locking in nutrients that are lost in other cooking methods like boiling too, so chips in moderation are better for you than you might think.

TERRY'S TWICE-FRIED CHIPS

Terry Adamson, Lewsey Lou's, St Agnes

Heading up the kitchen team at the Driftwood Spars in St Agnes, Terry oversees both the seafood restaurant and the fish and chip shop across the road. His tips will turn home-cooked chips into the stuff of summer holiday daydreams.

- Cut your chips on the chunky side, leaving the skins on for a rustic effect and flavour.
- In a deep fat fryer, blanch the chips in vegetable oil at 120°C for 7 minutes then dry and cool on kitchen paper – this will create that coveted fluffy centre. You can chill them at this point for finishing later if you like.
- Heat the oil to 180°C and fry the chips again for 6-7 minutes to create the golden crispy outer layer.
- Lift the chips from the fryer, giving them a good shake to drain them, toss in flaked Cornish sea salt and serve immediately.

KNOW YOUR TATERS

CORNISH SOIL IS RICH AND FERTILE, AND EVERY YEAR THE COUNTY'S POTATO GROWERS COVER THE EQUIVALENT OF **5000 FOOTBALL PITCHES** WITH THEIR CROP.

AROUND 1,000 HECTARES GET TURNED INTO CRISPS BUT, LUCKY FOR US, A FEW ALSO MAKE IT TO THE CHIP FRYER.

FISH 'N TIPS   Cornish Maris Piper potatoes are perfect for lighter, fluffier chips, with year-round quality.

WORTH ITS SALT

The sea surrounding Cornwall has supported livelihoods and lifestyles for many a century, but look deeper into the blue and there's more than fish to be found.

Harvested from the clean, crystal-clear waters off Cornwall's Lizard Peninsula, Cornish sea salt is as pure as it comes, with a mineral content that is utterly unique. The Lizard isn't just on the bucket list for Poldark fans and coast-path walkers - it's the only place in the world by the sea to harbour the particular mineral and geo-structure that makes the salt taste so good. With its crumbly, melt-in-the-mouth texture, it's no wonder Cornish sea salt has become the new culinary staple in kitchens from TR1 to NYC.

It's made by pumping pure seawater through state of the art, energy-efficient filters, simply crystallising a concentrated brine solution into its characteristic light, coarse crumbs.

The age when every coastal community in Cornwall made its own salt had long gone when the late Tony Fraser, founder of Cornish Sea Salt, brought the concept back to the Lizard in 2004. Tony spent three years finding the perfect location for producing the purest, mineral-rich salt, harvested straight from the Cornish sea. Just over a decade later, Cornish Sea Salt sits in kitchens across 26 countries, and is on the ingredients list of everything from high-end ready meals to luxury cosmetics.

WHAT TO USE WHEN

A guide to Cornish Sea Salt's most fish-friendly salts...

ORIGINAL

Deliciously uncomplicated, all those minerals from the clear Atlantic sea give a wonderfully intense flavour - so you don't use as much when you season your food.

FLAKED

Crumbly, delicate flakes - the perfect finishing salt, ideal for fries and canapés.

LEMON & THYME

Sea salt with lemon, thyme, onion and garlic. Delicious sprinked over white fish like pollack, hake or haddock.

FIERY SEA PEPPER

A spicy blend of seaweeds, chillies, peppercorns and sea salt. Perfect sprinkled over barbecued Cornish sardines.

SEAWEED SEA SALT

A nutritious duo of wakame seaweed and sea salt flakes - the yin and yang of the sea. Use to invigorate steamed and baked fish dishes.

SMOKED SEA SALT

Flakes of sea salt slowly smoked over apple and cherry wood chips for a naturally sweet smoky flavour; great with oilier fish like Cornish mackerel.

YEGHES DA!

The Cornish drinks scene is one of fizzing creativity and fabulous flavours, and a well-matched beverage with some fresh-as-it-gets Cornish seafood can nudge your eating experience from good to downright sublime. Here are a few pointers to get you raising the right glass, whatever you're tucking into…

1. SMEATONS
St Ives Cider

A crisp, clear, dry cider with a light sparkle that brings out the flavours of freshly pressed Cornish apples. Drink as an alternative to wine with any white fish dish. 6.5% ABV.

2. LERRYN BOATHOUSE CIDER
Haye Farm Cider

Fresh and fruity, this dry, traditionally-produced cider has a lovely appley acidity that cuts perfectly through oilier fish such as mackerel, mullet or bream. 5.2% ABV.

3. PEAR CIDER
Cornish Orchards

A light and delicate cider that rounds off the flavours of meatier fish dishes. Try it in a fluted glass with a lobster salad. 5% ABV.

4. VINTAGE CIDER
Fowey Valley Cider

A sparkling brut cider with a buttery flavour that goes amazingly well - not surprisingly - with Fowey moules marinière, both in the sauce and in the glass. 7.5% ABV.

5. REDCURRANT MEAD

Ninemaidens Mead

The almost sherry-like qualities of this mead, which has a redcurrant bite on the finish, make it a great partner for shellfish, particularly scallops. 12.5% ABV.

6. RONDO PINOT NOIR ROSÉ

Polgoon Vineyard and Orchard

A medium-dry, vibrant rosé from vineyards overlooking St Michael's' Mount, with a crisp acidity and strawberry flavours that partner beautifully with the sweetness of fresh Cornish crab. 11% ABV.

7. ATLANTIC DRY

Camel Valley

Cool, smooth, and crystal clear as the Cornish sea, this stunning white wine is perfect with more delicate fish such as plaice or megrim. 11.9% ABV.

8. KNIGHTOR BACCHUS 2013

Knightor Winery

A little like a classic Sauvignon Blanc, with aromas of citrus and cut grass which balance refreshingly well with the lightness of white fish. 11.15% ABV.

9. CORNISH PASTIS

South Western Distillery

A lingering pastis with flavours of Cornish gorse and citrus mingling with the characteristic aniseed. Ideal as a long apertif or short digestif before or after a fish supper; or try incorporating it into a rich bisque or cataplana stew. 42% ABV.

YEGHES DA
Cornish for good health

1. GLASNEY COLLEGE PORTER

Granite Rock Brewery

With a name inspired by the heritage of the ancient granite harbour town of Penryn, the smoky liquorice flavours of this rich, silky-smooth porter go down a treat with a plate of fresh Cornish oysters. 5.4% ABV.

2. PORTHLEVEN

Skinner's Brewery

A malty pale ale with citrussy notes, this easy session beer is the ideal partner for a beachside barbecue of tasty, freshly caught mackerel or sardines. 4.8% ABV.

3. LEWSEY LOU'S

Driftwood Spars Brewery

Brewed especially to complement the menu of the classy seafood takeaway next door to the brewery, try this biscuity copper bitter with fresh crab cakes or goujons. 3.8% ABV.

4. SWIFTIES LAGER

Keltek Brewery

A crisp, savoury lager with a cheeky acidity that cuts right through fattier fish dishes. Perfect with Cornish fish and chips. 4% ABV.

YOUR ROUND?

5. CHALKY'S BITE

Sharp's Brewery

A collaborative creation between Sharp's Brewery and Rick Stein, Chalky's is a succulent thirst-quencher, with notes of sweetness and fennel that make it perfect with oilier fish. 6.8% ABV.

6. CLOUDED YELLOW

St Austell Brewery

A flavoursome wheat beer with powerful notes of cloves and coriander that really enhance the intense, fragrant flavours of Goan and Bengali style seafood curries. 4.8% ABV.

7. MAY DAY

Padstow Brewing Company

Tropical flavours abound in this easy-drinking extra pale ale, brewed to coincide with Padstow's May Day celebrations. Great with a full-flavoured fish dish such as tacos. 5% ABV.

8. PILSNER

Harbour Brewing Company

Light enough to ensure the more subtle flavours of white fish come through, the hop combinations make this pilsner perfect alongside citrus and fennel-infused seafood and creamy fish dishes. 4.9% ABV.

Head off the beaten track with some much-loved Cornish beers, ales and lagers that will make your seafood really sing...

BUCKING THE MARKET

No-one could disagree that fishing is a proper way to make a living. Proper hard graft that is. But the rewards are sometimes scant. In common with farming, the harsh commercial reality of the rule of supply and demand means that, as rewarding as a plentiful catch can be, it won't necessarily make a fisherman rich. In fact, it might just send prices plummeting at market.

It's not an easy trend to buck, but a bit of creative thinking by some of Cornwall's entrepreneurial fishermen is beginning to do just that, by shaking up the way fish is being sold.

For a group of Newlyn day boats, it was the opportunity to harness the power of social media that prompted them to set up their collaborative venture, Dreckly Fish. Working their four boats collectively to catch a variety of species, they started by simply snapping the high-quality specimens coming over the side of their boats with their phones, posting the images on Twitter, and waiting for the orders to roll in. Chefs soon cottoned on and, after just two years, the group has regular customers willing to buy whatever they catch. Now they use social media as a way of showing customers the provenance and quality of the catch and letting chefs know what type of fish is on the way.

DRECKLY a well-loved term used in Cornwall to describe an unspecified time in the future. Think 'mañana' – only more laid back.

When fisherman Saul Astrinsky and his wife Abi set up Hayle-based business Wild Harbour as a way to cut out the middleman, it was always about getting a fair price for the fish. Fed up with seeing Saul's fish sold at market for prices they weren't happy with, they started offering his catch direct to chefs and fishmongers looking for premium, sustainably caught, day boat fish.

As demand grew, they started buying from other boats that could offer the same kind of quality, making the brave move of guaranteeing a set price for each species of fish for the whole of each season. This way, the fishermen know what they will receive for their catch before they've even landed it. Saul and Abi now buy from more than 20 Cornish boats and Saul's only regret is that he's too busy to go fishing himself these days.

Many of Cornwall's coastal communities evolved entirely around fishing, with shore-side jobs like packing and curing the catch or building and maintaining the fleet and gear just as important as the fishing itself. This is exactly how it was in the village of Mevagissey, where fortunes waxed and waned with the state of the fishery.

As the wheels of industry turned, the fishing continued almost everywhere but, particularly in some of the more remote and inaccessible harbours, it lost its place as the lifeblood of the community.

Not so in Meva. Thanks to some innovative thinking, today the fishing is booming; fish to the tune of around £2 million are landed each year, making it the fourth most important Cornish port after Newlyn, Padstow and Looe. A savvy approach to investment in boats and facilities is attracting a new generation of fishermen, some still teenagers who are keen for a foot on the fishing ladder, and there's a waiting list for moorings. These days it's a flexible fleet too, mostly day boats that can use the latest equipment to switch their gear according to the seasons and conditions, targeting top quality, high value fish all year that fetch good prices at market and from the merchants who buy direct from the boats. This is 21st century fishing in an ancient setting - and everyone's a winner.

PORT
OUT
STARBOARD
HOME

POSH FISH

Seafood's fresh taste and boundless versatility mean it's not only the perfect quick-prep crowdpleaser, but a few tweaks and touches will ensure it's also the centrepiece of a serious showstopper for sharing with friends.

From the relaxed simplicity of a few simple ingredients to pushing the boat out to impress, fish dishes can have style and adventure written all over them - think lighter-than-air scallops, a rich garlicky seafood stew with a kick, or impossibly pretty canapés - and you're on the right lines. Master these and prepare to savour not just the flavour, but the warm glow of admiration too.

This dish is easily adaptable so don't be afraid to try different things. Thinly sliced cooked pancetta or Parma ham work really well with scallops.

SCALLOPS WITH PEA PURÉE AND ROAST LEMON CRÈME FRAÎCHE

Ben Arthur, Fistral Beach Hotel and Spa, Newquay

Sweet, succulent and gorgeous to look at, scallops are a good place for anyone who thinks they don't like fish to start because their texture and flavour are not very 'fishy' at all. Cornish scallops are available all year and are collected either by diving or dredging. Cornwall's scallop-dredging industry is one of the most well-managed, with restrictions to minimise long-term damage to the seabed.

In this simple, elegant recipe, Ben makes the most of fresh, zesty flavours to contrast the sweetness of the scallops.

INGREDIENTS Serves 4

12 fresh Cornish scallops (with their coral)

200g freshly podded peas (or frozen)

I handful fresh mint leaves, finely chopped

I tbsp extra virgin olive oil

I lemon

I tsp sugar

100ml Cornish crème fraîche

Cooking oil

Cornish sea salt and black pepper

METHOD

FOR THE PEA PURÉE

- In a large pan, bring 2-3 litres of water to the boil, add the peas, cook for 1 minute, drain and lay them out on a large flat tray to cool. When cooled, put them in a blender with the mint and olive oil and blend until smooth. Season to taste with Cornish sea salt and ground black pepper and pass through a fine sieve using a spatula or the back of a spoon, creating a fine, smooth purée.

FOR THE CRÈME FRAÎCHE

- Grate the zest of the lemon into a bowl, taking care not to get any of the bitter white pith in there. Cut the lemon in half and slice off the ends so they will stand up in an ovenproof tray lined with parchment. Sprinkle the sugar over the flesh side of the lemon and bake at 170°C for 15-20 minutes. Remove from the oven and allow to cool.

- Add the crème fraîche to the bowl with the lemon zest and squeeze the roasted lemons through a fine sieve onto the mixture. Mix it to incorporate the juice whilst taking care not to over-whip it (you'll end up with butter); it should be nice and loose. Season to taste.

NOW FOR THE SCALLOPS

- They should be at room temperature before you cook them so they won't be cold in the centre. Heat a non-stick sauté pan until it is very hot. Coat the scallops with a little cooking oil, place in the pan and cook on a medium heat for about 2 minutes each side until golden. Lay them on a piece of kitchen towel to remove any excess oil. Place a tablespoonful of the pea purée on a clean plate and, with the back of the spoon, swipe through the purée so it creates a little nook and place the scallops in it. Drizzle some of the crème fraîche over and around the scallops. Finish the dish with pea shoots if you can get them.

 The orange part of the scallop, known sometimes as the coral, is in fact the roe.

JOHN DORY ROASTED WITH LEMON AND THYME

Emily Scott, St Tudy Inn, near Wadebridge

Firm and tasty, John Dory (a fish that derives its name from the subject of an old English ballad) is highly-prized for its meatiness and versatility. In this laid-back recipe, Emily keeps it simple, roasting the fish swiftly with minimal fuss and just a few classic ingredients.

> "John Dory is characterful and a joy to cook with."

INGREDIENTS Serves 2

4 small John Dory, filleted (ask your fishmonger)

A drizzle of olive oil

1 lemon

A few sprigs of fresh thyme leaves

Cornish sea salt and black pepper

METHOD

- Set the oven at 220°C.
- Put the John Dory in an oiled roasting tin. Season each fillet with salt and black pepper and drizzle generously with olive oil.
- Cut the lemon into six or so segments and tuck these, with the thyme leaves, underneath and in between the fillets.
- Roast for 10–12 minutes until the flesh is opaque. Serve on to warmed plates and spoon the lemon-scented olive oil juices over the fish.
- Chunks of fresh warm sourdough to mop up the juices would be perfect. A raw spinach and rocket salad with lemon zest and wholegrain dressing would be delicious with it too.

CORNISH HAKE WITH A SCALLOP GRATIN

Matthew Rowe, Falmouth Packet Inn, Rosudgeon

This dish is lovely for early spring when the first Cornish earlies are arriving but the winter greens are still around.

INGREDIENTS Serves 4

4 Cornish hake loin steaks, 180g each

4 fresh Cornish scallops with coral

8 slices of Cornish coppa ham

100g grated fresh parmesan

225ml Cornish double cream

16 Cornish new potatoes, par-boiled and cut in half

400g mixed greens (savoy, kale and spinach), lightly blanched

2 tbsp Cornish rapeseed oil

Cornish sea salt and pepper

METHOD

- For each gratin, press 2 slices of the ham into a small bun tin, place the scallop meats into each one and season. Mix the cream and parmesan together and spoon over the scallops. Place the tins on a tray in the oven at 200°C and cook for 5 minutes. Switch the oven off and leave the tray in the oven. Place four dinner plates in the oven to warm.

- Heat a non-stick, ovenproof pan and add a little oil. Season the hake and place in the pan skin side down for 4 minutes or until the skin is crispy and golden. Turn the fish and cook for a further 3 minutes, remove the fish and place in the warm oven to rest.

- Add the potatoes to the pan and fry on a high heat until they begin to brown. Add the greens and transfer to the oven for 3 or 4 minutes while you prepare to plate up.

- Remove the plates and the potatoes and greens from the oven and press a quarter of the vegetable mixture into a ring on the centre of each plate. Remove the ring, place the fish portions skin side up on top of the veg.

- Remove the gratins from their tin, place them on top of the fish and away you go.

FISH 'N TIPS You can also try serving this dish with a tomato, olive and basil sauce to add a summery flavour to it.

Hake is one of the most underrated fish in Britain and historically most of the hundreds of tonnes of hake landed in Cornwall each year ended up in Spain, where people love it. Cornish hake is the first in the UK to have received Marine Stewardship Council (MSC) accreditation, meaning that people can now look for the familiar MSC logo to be certain they are buying hake from a well managed sustainable fishery.

The white flesh of hake is quite soft but firms up on cooking, with a hint of sweetness, especially if really fresh. Because it's a large fish it comes in substantial chunks, so try using it in place of salmon or cod steaks or cutlets in recipes.

PYSK Cornish for fish

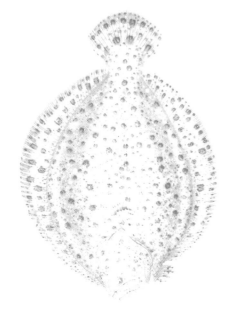

LIFE OF A GILL NETTER

A typical off-shore gill netter will go out for several days at a time, journeying many miles out to sea and dropping their nets for three days before being hauled in. For Simon Porter, skipper of the 21 metre netter 'Karen of Ladram', gill netting is a way of life. Heading out with his crew on the neap tides every two weeks, he catches hake, turbot and monkfish on two sets of specialist nets. The fish are landed at Newlyn where they head straight to the fish market.

Favoured by many of the larger Cornish fishing boats as a low-impact method of catching bigger volumes of fish, gill netting uses a fixed vertical panel of netting that hangs in the water using floats and weights –

imagine an underwater tennis net and you're on the right lines. Fish swim into it and if they're the right size they'll get trapped in the mesh. Small fish can swim straight through and escape, while species such as sharks and dolphins simply 'bounce' off.

The net is winched in and the fish are collected one by one, saving them from the crush and damage that can occur in a trawl net, and increasing their value at market. By varying the depth of the net, the fishermen generally catch what they aim to catch and, with no dragging or heavy chains, it's gentler on the seabed too.

Revered by chefs the world over, wild turbot produces juicy, flavoursome steaks that pan-fry beautifully, along with chunky bones that are ideal for stock-making. Simon Porter's son Jamie is a chef who makes the most of turbot's hearty meatiness in this dish that deserves a special occasion.

TURBOT WITH SCALLOP & LOBSTER RAVIOLI AND A VANILLA REDUCTION

Jamie Porter

INGREDIENTS Serves 4

4 fillets of turbot, each weighing approx. 200g

8 scallops

RAVIOLI

300g '00' flour

3 eggs and 1 egg yolk

30ml olive oil

15g salt

VANILLA REDUCTION

1-2 vanilla pods

1 litre fish stock

400ml vermouth

1 shallot, peeled

30ml Chardonnay vinegar

30g unsalted Cornish butter

SCALLOP AND LOBSTER MOUSSE

Roe from the 8 scallops

Blanched meat from 1 lobster

300ml Cornish double cream

1 egg white

Pinch of cayenne pepper

1 tbsp lemon juice

Cornish sea salt to taste

METHOD

- Cut away the roe from each scallop along with the sinew that attaches it. Keep the roe to one side. Plunge the scallops into iced water for 10 seconds, cleaning off any sand or grit. Lay them up against each other on a tray covered with a towel so they hold a good shape.

- Blitz the flour in a food processor with the salt. Slowly add the eggs and yolk one by one, then the olive oil. Tip out the dough onto a well-floured surface. Knead for 5 minutes until smooth. Wrap in cling film and rest in the fridge for at least 2 hours.

- Make the sauce: blitz the vanilla pods with the wine and stock and transfer to a pan, along with the whole shallot. Boil to reduce the liquid to about 100ml, then pass through a fine sieve. Set aside.

- Make the mousse: blitz the scallop roe and lobster in a food processor to a fine paste. Beat the egg white in a bowl until stiff. Semi-whip the cream in its own bowl then fold into the egg white with the lobster paste. Add the lemon juice, cayenne pepper and salt.

- Make the ravioli: using a pasta machine, roll your pasta out until you reach a 1.5 setting. (see page 98 for detailed pasta-making instructions) Alternatively, use a rolling pin to roll out your pasta in sections on a floured surface until it is the thickness of a 20p. Cut the pasta into an even number of discs about 8cm across (cut around a glass if you don't have a cutter this size).

- Put a tablespoon of the mousse in the middle of a disc, then slightly wet the edges and place another disc on top. Without squashing the mousse, seal the edges of the disc, gently pushing out any air. Repeat with the remaining discs and leave them on a floured surface. Bring a pan of salted water to the boil, and cook the parcels for 3 minutes each, removing them with a slotted spoon.

- Meanwhile, grill or pan-fry the turbot fillets with a little oil in a non-stick pan so they are really crisp on one side, then put aside and keep hot. In the same pan, fry off the scallops until just cooked.

- Pop the vanilla sauce back on the heat then whisk in the butter and Chardonnay vinegar and warm through.

- Arrange the turbot, scallops and ravioli on warmed plates, before drizzling over the sauce.

- Perfect served with a light summer vegetable ratatouille.

CORNISH FISH STEW WITH CRAB & 'NDUJA TOAST

Andy Appleton, Fifteen Cornwall, Watergate Bay

This sumptuous low-maintenance stew, enhanced by the fiery kick of the 'Nduja, could be scaled up or down for a family feast or a quiet supper for two.

INGREDIENTS Serves 4 to 6

20g dried sea spaghetti

1 red pepper

1 yellow pepper

3 tbsp Cornish rapeseed oil

1 medium leek, cleaned and sliced

1 small fennel bulb, sliced

Pinch of crushed dried chillies

2 cloves of garlic, finely chopped

300g cherry tomatoes

500ml fish stock

250g cockles, cleaned

500g mussels, cleaned

500g mixed firm white fish (gurnard, monkfish, sea bass or whatever is in season), cut into small chunks

300g squid, cleaned and sliced

Small bunch of flat leaf parsley, chopped

Zest of 1 unwaxed lemon

Cornish sea salt and pepper

FOR THE 'NDUJA TOAST

4 to 6 small slices of toast

30g 'Nduja

80g handpicked white crab meat

'Nduja is a spreadable, spicy pork sausage from Italy, and is available from some larger supermarkets or online.

METHOD

- Put the dried sea spaghetti into a mixing bowl, cover with tepid water and leave to soak for 30 minutes. Drain, cut into slightly shorter lengths if necessary, and drop into a pan of boiling water. Cook for 10 minutes, then drain, rinse and set to one side.

- Preheat the oven to 220°C. Rub the peppers with oil and roast them in the oven for 20-25 minutes until soft and slightly blackened. Seal inside a plastic bag, leave to cool, then break them open and remove and discard the stalks, seeds and skin. Cut the flesh into strips and set to one side.

- Heat the rapeseed oil in a large, deep pan over a medium heat. Add the leek, fennel, chilli and garlic and gently fry until just soft. Add the cherry tomatoes and when the tomatoes are soft and squishy, pour in the stock and bring to the boil. Now add the seaweed, cockles and mussels and when these start to open (after about 1 minute), add the squid and the white fish and simmer for another 3 minutes. When all the seafood is cooked, add the lemon zest (a little lemon juice to taste), the cooked peppers and the chopped parsley. Season to taste and serve.

- Spread the 'Nduja on the toast, top with crab, and serve alongside the stew.

ROASTED COD FILLET
WITH PRAWN ANGLAISE

Ryan Venning, Porthminster Beach Café, St Ives

Anyone would be forgiven for thinking it's a sin to buy cod. The truth is that, as with so many other fish, it's fine to buy cod as long as you know it's been caught in a sustainable way. At certain times of year, fantastic cod is caught off the Cornish coast, worth looking out for and turning into a special treat.

INGREDIENTS Serves 4

4 cod fillet portions, approx. 170g each, skinned

75g Cornish salted butter

200g British or North Atlantic prawns, cooked and peeled

4 shallots, peeled and finely chopped

1 clove garlic, peeled and finely chopped

200ml fish stock

200ml Cornish double cream

Pinch of cayenne pepper

Ground white pepper

Cornish sea salt

METHOD

- Heat the oven to 170°C. Season each cod portion with white pepper and wrap them individually in foil parcels, laying a thin slice of the butter on top and underneath each piece of fish before sealing. Place in an ovenproof dish and roast for 20-25 minutes.

- For the prawn sauce, melt a good knob of the remaining butter in a pan. Add the shallots and garlic and sweat down gently until they are transparent. Do not let them brown.

- Add the prawns and stock to the pan. Bring to the boil and simmer until reduced by about one third. Add the cream, boil and reduce again until the sauce coats the back of a wooden spoon.

- Season to taste with white pepper, salt and a hint of cayenne pepper, then blend until smooth (a stick blender is ideal). Pass through a fine sieve or chinois to ensure the sauce is velvety smooth.

- Remove the cod from the oven, unwrap and place on warm plates. Pour the sauce over generously.

- Serve with crisp, roasted, sliced potato 'coins' and seasonal veg.

ONE BITE WONDERS

Impressing guests at any gathering with little mouthfuls of concentrated seafood deliciousness is easier than you might think. And not a vol au vent in sight if you follow these suggestions, which use good value, sustainable Cornish fish.

SPIDER CRAB SCRAPS WITH CRISPY SEAWEED

Jah Hemming, Knightor Winery, near St Austell

Crispy bits of tempura batter coated flakes of crab work well with any hard shell crab meat but in early summer and late autumn look out for the spider crabs that come into Cornish waters. Gutweed is the bright green slimy wet grass-like seaweed found attached to rockpools. Using it lightly dried and fried means there's no need to add extra salt.

INGREDIENTS

125g self raising flour

125g cornflour

250g mixed white and brown crab meat

Ice-cold sparkling water, wine, cider, or beer/lager

A handful of gutweed – use scissors when harvesting to protect the root

Malt vinegar

Oil for frying

FISH 'N TIPS

Try the vinegar made in the old nuclear bunker in the Cornish village of Coverack

METHOD

- Lightly dry the gutweed between tea towels in a low oven or in the sun to avoid it spitting when cooking. Drop into a deep fryer at 180°C for 10 seconds or until translucent. Set aside on kitchen paper to drain.

- Working quickly in small batches, put a tablespoon each of the two flours and crab meat in a bowl and add enough sparkling liquid to make a batter the consistency of thick double cream.

- While the bubbles are still present, drizzle the batter from the end of a spoon into the deep fryer. Remove when the scraps are golden brown and set aside on kitchen paper.

- Repeat until all the mixture is used.

- Season to taste with black pepper and the crispy seaweed and splash with malt vinegar. Serve in baking parchment cones.

SEA BREAM TARTARE WITH PICKLED SEA SANDWORT

Sea bream is a good sustainable alternative to bass with a smaller flake texture. Sea sandwort is a small succulent found near the coast. Pickled, it has a cucumber-like taste. The combination of the two yields one classy mouthful.

INGREDIENTS Serves 4 or more

1 very fresh filleted sea bream, skinned and finely diced

1 spring onion, finely chopped

½ an apple, finely diced

Drizzle of Cornish rapeseed oil

Cornish sea salt and black pepper

1 tsp each chopped parsley and chives

2 tsp chopped pickled sandwort or cucumber, plus pickle juice (or use gherkins)

METHOD

- Chop the pickled sandwort or cucumber into small pieces.
- Mix all the ingredients together apart from the pickles and herbs. Season to taste.
- Heap the mixture onto dessert spoons and garnish with the pickles, herbs and a little pickle juice. Serve straight away.

IN A PICKLE?

You can quickly pickle cucumber by pouring warm vinegar over it. Or try this easy technique Jah picked up from forager Rachel Lambert for pickling sea sandwort:

- Cover the sea sandwort with vinegar and bring to the boil.
- Pour into sterile jars and seal.
- Leave in a cool place for a month before using.

FISHING SPIRIT

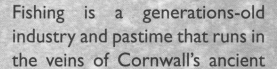

Fishing is a generations-old industry and pastime that runs in the veins of Cornwall's ancient character, influencing everything from feasts, festivals, tales and traditions to shanties, sermons and superstitions. Whether you're a born and bred native, just passing through, or have never crossed the Tamar in your life, the Cornish spirit is downright infectious. It'll draw you in, wrap you up and keep you coming back for more.

For centuries; and for centuries to come, the fishing industry has been a bedrock on which many Cornish communities subsist, thrive, mourn and celebrate in a way that aptly honours the energy of those who live and breathe the real saltwater lifestyle. It's the spirit that makes the Mousehole cat purr, a coastal neighbourhood rally together in tougher times, and the fiercest of men raise his glass and sing along in raucous harmony.

The fishing spirit is in the blood.

F**i**sh Feasts

Cornish folk have never needed much encouragement to party, and every coastal town and village would once have held an annual bash to celebrate getting through another year and set them in good stead for the next. Many of these had their origins in pagan customs that were adopted and adapted by the christian church.

Fish are still the focus of many of the coastal celebrations, which are a great way to learn more about seafood and try things you might not have tasted before – and a great day out of course.

CORNWALL'S

MARCH **Rick Stein's Beer and Mussel Festival, St Merryn** A weekend featuring Cornish ales and ciders and local mussels cooked to some of Rick's recipes.

MARCH/APRIL **Good Friday Trigging, Helford Estuary** An annual shoreline cockle-foraging tradition dating back hundreds of years.

JUNE **Mevagissey Fish Festival** Cornish fishing communities always celebrated St Peter, the Patron Saint of fishermen, on 29th June - St Peter's Day. In true Cornish style, this often turned into several days of celebration that became known as St Peter's-tide. Mevagissey is one of the few places where this link remains intact, with a day-long fish festival kicking off its historic Feast Week.

JULY **Mousehole Sea Salts and Sail (biennial)** A festival that includes the Tattyella Feast. Tattyella is the Cornish version of paella, made with potatoes, the staple Cornish carb, rather than the Spanish rice, but including the key ingredient, saffron, to produce the customary yellow colour. Some dare to claim that the recipe originated in Cornwall and was stolen by the Spanish when they ransacked the village in 1595.

JULY **Rock Oyster Festival** Music, food and camping to celebrate the oysters of the Camel estuary, near the village of Rock.

TROIL a Cornish word for a celebration similar to a ceilidh, which always ended the pilchard season. Each cellar had its own troil, consisting of a feast with games and dancing in the loft.

& FeStivaLs

—FISH FEST CALENDAR—

AUGUST **Newlyn Fish Festival** A Bank Holiday favourite for thousands of visitors each year in Cornwall's largest fishing port. Proceeds go to the Fishermen's Mission.

....

SEPTEMBER **Newquay Fish Festival** A three-day fish-filled event held on Newquay's historic working harbour.

....

SEPTEMBER **Great Cornish Food Festival** Held in the county town of Truro and the largest event anywhere dedicated entirely to Cornish food and drink. with plenty of ways to try, buy and learn about Cornish seafood.

....

OCTOBER **Falmouth Oyster Festival** A four-day festival celebrating a name now protected by the EU and an ancient tradition of harvesting wild native oysters using only sail or oar.

....

DECEMBER **Tom Bawcock's Eve, Mousehole** A pre-Christmas celebration of the Star Gazey Pie.

The most famous Cornish fish dish is the iconic Star Gazey Pie, a fish pie made with whole fish (usually sardines) with their heads poking through the pastry topping – gazing towards the stars. The exact origin of the dish is lost in the annals of time and is subject to typical controversy, but one fact that's certain is that the dish is associated with the fishing village of Mousehole, near Penzance. The story dates back to the 16th century and tells of a local fisherman, Tom Bawcock, who braved a terrible storm and landed an immense catch of fish as the village faced starvation just before Christmas. The fish were baked in an enormous pie for everyone to share, with the fish heads poking through to prove to the villagers that there really were fish inside.

Whether you believe the story or not, like so many other Cornish legends it has become a great excuse for a celebration. Every year, Mousehole celebrates Tom Bawcock's Eve – 23rd December – by making a giant Star Gazey Pie and parading it through the village, along with lanterns and singing, against the resplendent backdrop of Mousehole's famous Christmas lights. To try the pie, drop in to the Ship Inn, where you're guaranteed it will be on the menu every Tom Bawcock's Eve.

rry Night,

"Merry place you may believe, 'Tiz Mouzel 'pon Tom Bawcock's eve. To be there then who wouldn't wesh, to sup o' sibm soorts o' fish, When morgy brath has cleared the path, Comed lances for a fry, And then us had a bit o' scad an' Starry-gazie pie. As aich we'd drunk, E's health we'd drunk in bumpers brimmen high. And when up caame Tom Bawcock's name, We'd drink'd un to the sky."

The Starry Gazie Pie song, written by Robert Morton Nance in 1927. Sung on Tom Bawcock's Eve in Mousehole

STAR GAZEY PIES

Nathan Outlaw, Port Isaac

Nathan Outlaw's take on the traditional Star Gazey Pie recipe makes cute individual pies rather than a big one. He also uses mackerel rather than pilchards and leaves out the traditional potato and egg.

INGREDIENTS Serves 4

4 medium mackerel, gutted and butterflied, tails intact

PASTRY

250g plain flour, plus extra to dust

1 tsp fine Cornish sea salt

250g very cold butter, cut into cubes

About 125ml ice-cold water

Egg wash (1 egg yolk beaten with 2 tsp milk)

FILLING

50ml light Cornish rapeseed oil

3 rashers of smoked streaky bacon, derinded and diced

2 shallots, peeled and chopped

2 garlic cloves, peeled and chopped

40g plain flour

50ml Cornish cider vinegar

100ml Cornish cider

100ml fish stock

150g hog's pudding, diced

3 tsp chopped chives

Cornish sea salt and freshly ground black pepper

METHOD

- To make the pastry, combine the flour and salt in a bowl. Add the butter and rub in using your fingertips, until the butter cubes are smaller and the dough is grainy. Add enough water, a little at a time, to bring the dough together. Roll the dough into a ball, wrap in cling film and chill in the fridge for 20 minutes. Roll out the pastry on a lightly floured surface to a rectangle, about 30 x 20cm. Fold into three, as if folding a letter to go into an envelope. Turn the pastry 90° and roll out and fold as before, then wrap the pastry in cling film and chill for 30 minutes. Repeat the same two roll, fold and turns once more, then wrap and chill for a further 30 minutes. The pastry is now ready to roll.

- To make the filling, heat a saucepan over a medium heat and add the oil. When hot, add the diced bacon and cook for 4 minutes until golden. Add the shallots and garlic and cook for 2 minutes, stirring occasionally. Add the flour and cook, stirring, for a further 2 minutes. Now gradually add the cider vinegar, cider and fish stock, stirring as you go. Bring to the boil, lower the heat and simmer for 5 minutes, stirring occasionally to ensure it does not catch. Add the hog's pudding and chives, then take off the heat. Season with salt and pepper and divide between four individual pie dishes. Clean the edges of the dishes and leave to cool.

- Roll out the pastry into four ovals or rounds (large enough to cover the pie dishes) and put back into the fridge for 10 minutes to firm up.

- Heat your oven to 200°C. Cut the tails from the mackerel and set aside. Check the fish for any pin bones and season with salt and pepper. Lay the fillets on top of the cooled filling. Brush the rims of the dishes with egg wash and position the pastry lids over the filling. Trim away excess pastry but don't be too tidy – you're after a rustic look! Place them in the fridge until ready to cook. Bake the pies for 15-20 minutes until the pastry is golden.

- Cut a hole in the top of each pie and insert a fish tail. Pop back into the oven for 5 minutes, then serve immediately, with a green salad or vegetables.

"The heritage of fishing running through Cornwall is so strong that our fishermen are some of the most experienced there are, leading to them holding a great respect for both the sea and the fish thus ensuring that it comes to market in the best possible condition."

A love of cooking seafood is what drew the young Nathan Outlaw to Cornwall, with the ambition of working for Rick Stein. These days he's become one of the world's most highly acclaimed seafood chefs, whose intuitive preparation makes the fish the star on any plate.

DAVID LOFTUS

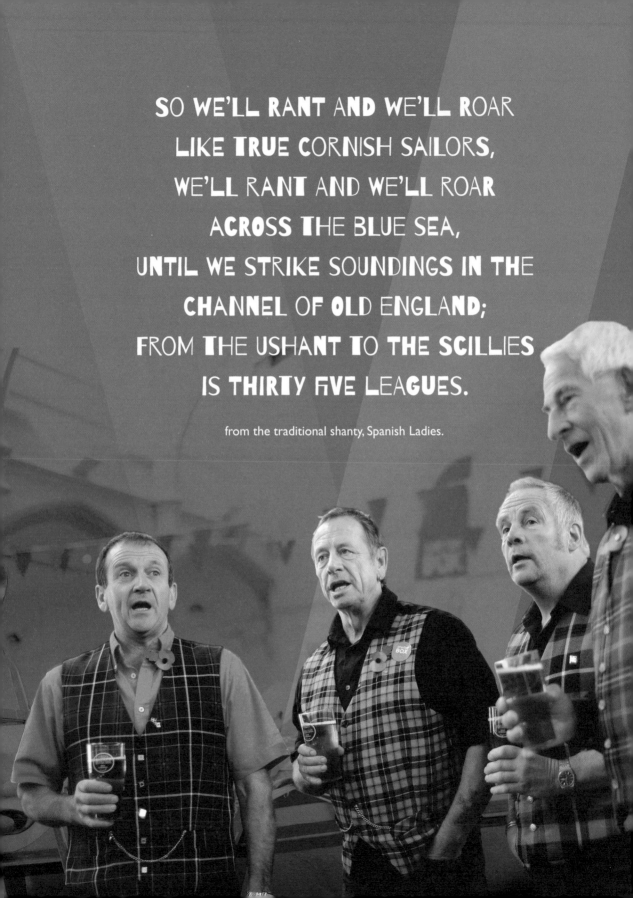

SO WE'LL RANT AND WE'LL ROAR
LIKE TRUE CORNISH SAILORS,
WE'LL RANT AND WE'LL ROAR
ACROSS THE BLUE SEA,
UNTIL WE STRIKE SOUNDINGS IN THE
CHANNEL OF OLD ENGLAND;
FROM THE USHANT TO THE SCILLIES
IS THIRTY FIVE LEAGUES.

from the traditional shanty, Spanish Ladies.

PULLING TOGETHER

Drop into a village pub anywhere in Cornwall on a Friday night and you might well come across a shout — a name far too harsh for the harmonies that pipe up, led by a few accomplished singers but open to anyone to join in. In fact, once a shout gets going, keeping quiet amongst the infectious goodwill and camaraderie, and the effects of a Cornish ale or two, is futile.

Shanties are often thought of as the songs of fishermen, but in fact hark back to the days of sailing, where jobs like hauling massive canvasses and heavy anchors depended on a rhythm to keep the crew pulling together. Cornish shanty-singing today combines the sailing songs of old with some of the traditional songs and hymns that originated at a time when music was the main form of entertainment for communities who toiled long and hard out at sea, down the mines and in the fields.

A highspot in the Cornish shanty singing calendar is the Falmouth International Sea Shanty Festival held each year in June and described as the largest free festival of maritime music on the planet. Three days of song and high spirits in aid of the RNLI.

TALL TALES & FAR-FETCHED FOLKLORE

Long days and nights on an unpredictable ocean mean superstitions abound on board the boat, and many fishermen still firmly hold beliefs that are centuries old, passed from generation to generation.

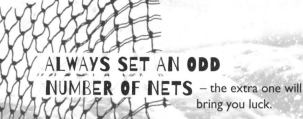

ALWAYS SET AN ODD NUMBER OF NETS – the extra one will bring you luck.

Stick to apples and pears – a banana on board is bad luck.

Haul your nets on the starboard side, <u>NEVER</u> the port side.

RABBITS ARE BAD NEWS – crew members mustn't say the word 'rabbit' on board the boat, and if rabbits are spotted in the fields as you're setting out, you should turn around and go back to port.

FISHING BOATS SHOULD BE PAINTED ANY COLOUR <u>BUT</u> GREEN – it's considered very bad luck.

IT'S BAD LUCK TO LAUNCH A NEW BOAT OR START A NEW FISHING SEASON ON A FRIDAY.

WHISTLING ON BOARD IS A NO-NO

(Tell your partner not to whistle while you're away, as it will cause a storm at sea!)

Fasten your chinstrap

- losing a hat overboard means you're in for a long trip.

" Pass salt, pass sorrow."

The salt pot mustn't be handed from one crewman to another, or there'll be bad luck.

If a clergyman wishes you well as you set out

– DON'T GO (they're the pagan sea gods' natural enemies).

WHEN A FISHERMAN SETS OFF...

...DON'T CALL OUT AFTER HIM ONCE HE SETS FOOT OUTSIDE THE FRONT DOOR.

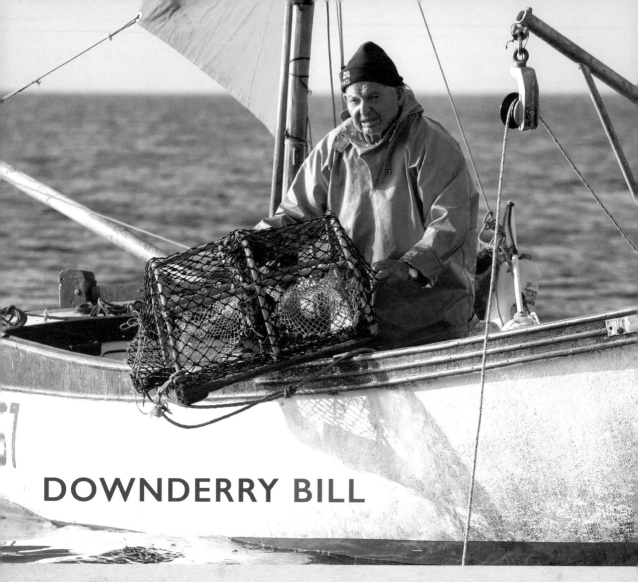

DOWNDERRY BILL

A gritty, raw existence entirely at the mercy of the elements and the markets isn't most people's idea of a dream job. That's why it takes a certain resolve to be a fisherman. And few could argue with the resolve of a man who's fished for 70 years, is still going to sea at the ripe age of 86, but claims he's never 'worked' in his life because he enjoys every minute.

That man is Bill Hocking - Downderry Bill to anyone around south east Cornwall - almost certainly the oldest commercial fisherman in Cornwall, and probably Britain. Bill fishes for crab and lobster and keeps his boat in Looe harbour these days; at the insistence of his wife Margaret, he gave up launching his boat from the shore at Downderry when he was 85.

Downderry was where it all began for Bill, arriving there during the war after his family was bombed out of their home in Plymouth, and taking to a little pram dinghy he was given like the proverbial duck to water.

He's seen a few changes since then of course, in a career that evolved into him becoming one of the south coast's most successful trawlermen (he gave up trawling when he was 80). He talks wistfully of an age when the best fishermen were those who developed a kind of sixth sense for the weather and the sea conditions and

"If you enjoy what you're doing, it isn't hard. It's better than being in an office looking at the clock."

recalls how important this became during the war, when radio weather forecasts were suspended yet fishermen were vital in keeping the nation fed.

Margaret has been at Bill's side for 62 of those 70 years at sea and, as well as helping launch the boats and land the catch, one of her jobs used to be to keep him supplied with two of her home-made meat and potato pasties (no onion or swede) every day. At one time his crew calculated that if all the pasties he'd eaten were lined up they would measure a mile and a half!

By his own confession he isn't an adventurous eater and, curiously, he doesn't like fish.

FOR THOSE IN PERIL ON THE SEA

Fishing is the most hazardous peacetime occupation in Britain and any fisherman's partner or mother will tell you that, even if they've learnt not to fill their lives with worry, the underlying anxiety about the dangers of the job never goes away. But nothing can ever prepare someone for the call they dread the most, yet somehow never expect to receive.

For Cornish MP Sheryll Murray, that call came as she was returning home by train one day from the Commons where, ironically, she had been lobbying about the importance of the Coastguard service. Little did she know at the time that, just a few hours later, the very service she was battling for would be helping in a search for her own husband, whose boat was overdue returning to Looe harbour.

Neil Murray was an accomplished seafarer. Growing up in South East Cornwall, he had always wanted to go to sea and, like many other fishermen, had worked his way up through the trade from a young age to become skipper of his own boat. Our Boy Andrew, a Cygnus 33 stern trawler built in Falmouth, was named after Sheryll and Neil's son and served them well. However, in 2005, with increasing pressure on financial viability, Neil decided he would need either to invest in a bigger boat or lose his crew and work Our Boy Andrew single-handed. He opted for the latter, but made an agreement with Sheryll not to work in bad weather.

Five years later, it wasn't a stormy sea that claimed Neil's life. There are plenty of other dangers in fishing and, in Neil's case, it was such a simple thing – a toggle on the hood of his oilskin getting caught in his net as he hauled it in – that caused another tragic accident at sea. With no-one on board to help and no emergency stop button on his gear, he became tangled in the net and suffered fatal injuries.

Hearing Sheryll describe the numbness she felt on learning Neil was missing, the frustration of waiting for news, her grief on finally hearing the words: 'he didn't make it' and the struggle of breaking the news to her children, it's hard to imagine how anyone copes. Sheryll's solution was to try to find a sense of purpose for what occurred and made it her mission to help reduce the chances of similar accidents happening again. She sent out a strong message to fishermen to cut the toggles from their hoods and to use grants that were available to install safety cut-outs on their gear.

Other fishermen's widows will readily agree that finding strength in those dark hours is an almighty task. Many will say it's the Fishermen's Mission that kept them going through the worst, providing someone outside the family who understands fishing to offer a hand to hold, take on practical challenges like paperwork, or simply just listen. They make life that bit more bearable for fishermen and their families in any time of need, not just when a life is lost.

This book is dedicated to all the fishermen who have lost their lives at sea and to all those who risk their lives to bring fish to our tables.

ACKNOWLEDGEMENTS

Heartfelt thanks to the very many people who have helped to shape and make the Great Cornish Fish Book:

Rosie Willmot, for inspired writing, sharp wit and keen eye.

Dave Huxley, Grace Lobb and Kevin Gray-Roberts, for knowledge, research, ideas, writing and proofing.

Emma Gordon and Sal Mitchell at Design Room Cornwall for stunning design, striking photography, great teamwork and endless patience.

Heather Allen, Sean Gee and Kate Whitaker for beautiful illustrations and photography.

Seafish for use of their extensive library of seafood illustrations.

Mark Rogers and the guys at Fourway Print for expert work and being so helpful.

Terry Adamson, Tor Amran, Andy Appleton, Ben Arthur, Abi and Saul Astrinsky, Tom Brown, Robert Bunny, Emilie Cole, Sarah Collins, Cornwall Good Seafood Guide, Selina Crookes, Sarah Crosbie, Caroline Davey, Bob Davidson, Mark Devonshire, Stewart and Anna Eddy, Nina Eyles, Kris Fleming, Heidi Fitzpatrick, Roger Forbes, Ben and Terry George, Chris Gilbertson, Chris Gordon, Will Gould, Calum Greenhalgh, Robin Hancock, Jo Harris, Zack Hawke, Neil Haydock, Sarah Hayes, Jah Hemming, Bill and Margaret Hocking, Brian Johnston, Adam Land, James Land, Rosie Land, Nigel Legge, Chloe Marsland, Dale McIntosh, Sophia Medine, Gary Mitchell, Sheryll Murray, Johnny Murt, National Lobster Hatchery, Nathan Outlaw, Sharon Outlaw, Rob Parsons, George Pascoe, Amanda Pender, Angela and Jackie Pengelly, Kevin Penney, Matt Perry, Rob Poole, Jamie Porter, Simon Porter and the crew of Karen of Ladram, Bernie Powling, Chris Ranford, Gary and Marina Rawle, Chris Richards, Paul Ripley, Matthew Rowe, Steve Ryman, Emily Scott, David Seabourne, Joan Shiles, Belinda Shipp, Annie Sibert, Matt Slater, Chris Smallwood, Isobel Smith, Jo Smith, Clare Stanley, Jack Stein, Rick Stein, Mark Sullivan, Philip Tanswell, Lindsey Thomas, Valerie and Charlotte Thomson, Rick Toogood, Lee Trigger, Ben Tunnicliffe and the staff at Ben at Sennen, Ryan Venning, Claire Vickers, Fiona Were, Jon and Vicki Crwys-Williams, Rob Wing - for sharing their time, insights, recipes, photographs and guidance.

And everyone else within and around the fishing and seafood industry of Cornwall and the Isles of Scilly. You do a fantastic job.

Ruth Huxley, August 2015

FV767